DR. PA

Heaven

OR Hell

...Your Choice

Unveiling Divine Revelations

SECOND EDITION

ISBN: 9781936989195

Library of Congress Control Number: 2011934741

Published by
NewBookPublishing.com, a division of Reliance Media, Inc.
515 Cooper Commerce Drive, #140, Apopka, FL 32703
NewBookPublishing.com

Printed in the United States of America

Book Dedication

This book is dedicated to the glory, honor, and praise of
My Papa Father God
My Sweet Jesus
My Precious Holy Spirit
Who intimately knows me and lavishly loves me.
LORD GOD,
You are my life and my breath.
I love You with all of my heart.
Thank You from the depths of my spirit for these
amazing visions and rich treasures from Your Word.
Your Handmaiden,
Patricia

Table of Contents

Dedication 3

Prologue 7

Introduction 9

Part One - Hell

Chapter One - Gates to Hell 13

Chapter Two – Location of Hell 21

Chapter Three – Belly of Hell 27

Chapter Four – Legs of Hell 31

Chapter Five – The Bottomless Pit 41

Chapter Six – Lake of Fire 47

Chapter Seven – Who's in Hell? 51

Chapter Eight- Demons and Spirits 63

Chapter Nine – Schemes of Satan 73

Part Two – Heaven

Chapter Ten – Gate to Heaven 105

Chapter Eleven – Location of Heaven 117

Chapter Twelve – The Record Room 127

Chapter Thirteen – The Fellowship Room 137

Chapter Fourteen – The Prayer Room 145

Chapter Fifteen– The Throne Room 165

Chapter Sixteen – The Banquet Room 185

Chapter Seventeen – Who's in Heaven? 191

Chapter Eighteen – Angels and Messengers 197

Conclusion 221

Epilogue 229

Prologue

Sweetly surrounded by His glorious presence during my pure time of worship, I was given a vision that opened up as a beautiful flower unfolds its petals to reveal its splendor. In this marvelous vision, I was kneeling at the feet of Jesus while He reclined comfortably in a chair. The Lord Jesus was speaking Aramaic to me, and I understood the language, even though I had never learned it. I listened intently as Jesus explained certain things. Then the Lord Jesus placed His right hand on my head and said: ***"Go forth, for I send you. Do not fear, My child, for I am with you."*** I stood and gazed intently into Jesus' reassuring eyes and then turned to go. I knew my mission; it had been sealed by the hand of God.

The mission imparted to me through Jesus Christ is to preach God's truth so that people can be set free. "Therefore if the Son makes you free, you shall be free indeed" (John 8:36). There are many people who are trapped by the bondage of the enemy, which prevents them from experiencing this great liberty God has for them. Satan began his deceit in the Garden of Eden when he said to Eve, "Did God really say not to eat of the fruit of this tree? Surely you will not die if you eat from it."

Satan continues his deception upon mankind when he says: "There is no heaven and there is no hell. When you die, it is over and there is no life after death." Or Satan whispers in the ear of those who do believe in heaven and hell, "There are many ways to heaven, just do what is right in your own eyes and you will get there, because God loves you." Both are lies from the pit of hell.

Heaven is a real place that has been prepared by God for those who have repented of their sins and have asked Jesus to forgive them. Receiving Jesus' gift of salvation guarantees eternal life in heaven. Likewise, hell is a real place for those who have refused the gift of forgiveness through Jesus Christ's death and resurrection. Hell is not an exclusive place just for mass murderers, drug lords, and child-traffickers. Hell is made up of ordinary sinners. If you have ever told a lie, cheated on your income taxes, had lustful thoughts, become angry, used God's name as a swear word, then you are a sinner. Hell is your destination without Jesus.

My assignment from the Lord is to communicate His truth, because there are only two choices: heaven or hell. There are no other options, no matter what you have been taught, what you have heard, or what you believe. Ultimately, you decide which place you will spend eternity. My prayer is that you will come away with a greater biblical understanding of heaven and hell, and make a decision worthy of the knowledge you have gained through this book. For those who know Jesus and know their own heavenly destination, my prayer is that these spiritual visions and rich teachings that were imparted to me by the Holy Spirit will strengthen your walk with God and draw you ever closer to Jesus.

Introduction

The Holy Spirit woke me in the middle of the night and gave me the following message before I began writing this book: *"There is an invisible barrier that must be crossed to go into the spiritual realm. Angels freely cross this barrier to travel back and forth from heaven to earth and demons cross this barrier to travel from hell to earth because they are spirits. In order to cross this barrier, you will be in the spirit, but your body will remain on earth. You will see things in heaven and hell, but your physical body will remain on earth. You will have your five senses when you are in the spiritual realm and see these visions. You will be able to hear, see, smell, touch and taste. You will also have all your emotions: fear, anguish, sorrow, joy, peace and laughter."*

"When it is time for you to view heaven and hell, I will assign an angel to you. Angels have different jobs and functions, and they take orders from Me; they do not act alone. My angel will escort you into the spiritual realm. Do not fear. I am preparing you in advance so you know how it will happen. I will show you visions of heaven and hell so

you can record what you see for this book. My child, do you accept this commission I have set before you?" I answered the Lord, "Yes Lord God, I am Your handmaiden. I accept Your commission to go in the spirit to heaven and hell to record what I will witness for this book."

In the Bible, there are scriptural examples of people being taken in the Spirit to view things God wanted to show them. The Apostles John and Paul were taken up in the Spirit and shown things in heaven so they could record their experiences. "After these things I looked, and behold, a door standing open in heaven. And the first voice that I heard was like a trumpet speaking with me, saying, 'Come up here, and I will show you things which must take place after this.' Immediately I was in the Spirit; and behold, a throne set in heaven, and One sat on the throne" (Revelation 4:1-2). "It is doubtless not profitable for me to boast. I will come to visions and revelations of the Lord: I know a man in Christ who fourteen years ago— whether in the body I do not know, or whether out of the body I do not know, God knows—such a one was caught up to the third heaven. And I know such a man—whether in the body or out of the body I do not know, God knows— how he was caught up into Paradise and heard inexpressible words, which it is not lawful for a man to utter" (1 Corinthians 12:1-4). The Prophet Ezekiel was lifted in the Spirit to an unusual place so God's revelations could be recorded. "The hand of the LORD came upon me and brought me out in the Spirit of the LORD, and set me down in the midst of the valley; and it was full of bones. Then He caused me to pass by them all around, and behold, there were very many in the open valley; and indeed they were very dry" (Ezekiel 37:1-2).

I do not want to elevate or equate myself with these great Apostles and Prophets who were shown mighty things to record in the Bible; for I am just a humble handmaiden of the Lord. What I have learned and accepted is that God is sovereign and He has a purpose for revealing certain details about heaven and hell at this point in history. I believe that we are very close to entering the final years before Christ returns, but only the Father in heaven knows the time and the day. There are signs that we are approaching these last days and Jesus described to His disciples the sign of His coming and the end of the age.

> "And Jesus answered and said to them: 'Take heed that no one deceives you. For many will come in My name, saying, 'I am the Christ,' and will deceive many. And you will hear of wars and rumors of wars. See that you are not troubled; for all these things must come to pass, but the end is not yet. For nation will rise against nation, and kingdom against kingdom. And there will be famines, pestilences, and earthquakes in various places. All these are the beginning of sorrows.'"

> "Then they will deliver you up to tribulation and kill you, and you will be hated by all nations for My name's sake. And then many will be offended, will betray one another, and will hate one another. Then many false prophets will rise up and deceive many. And because lawlessness will abound, the love of

many will grow cold. But he who endures to the end shall be saved. And this gospel of the kingdom will be preached in all the world as a witness to all the nations, and then the end will come" (Matthew 24:4-14).

God's grace and mercy are demonstrated when people receive the great gift of salvation through Jesus Christ, and their eternal destination is heaven. God has magnanimously given me the privilege to be His mouthpiece of truth to people all over the world, and I am honored to be His handmaiden in writing His book about heaven and hell.

~ CHAPTER ONE ~

Gates to Hell

In the Old Testament, there was a place referred to as Tophet, or the Valley of the Son of Hinnom. This place was where the Israelites sacrificed their sons and daughters in the fire to a Canaanite god called Molech. "And they have built the high places of Tophet, which is in the Valley of the Son of Hinnom, to burn their sons and their daughters in the fire, which I did not command, nor did it come into My heart. ' Therefore behold, the days are coming,' says the LORD, 'when it will no more be called Tophet, or the Valley of the Son of Hinnom, but the Valley of Slaughter; for they will bury in Tophet until there is no room'" (Jeremiah 7:31-32). Isaiah also spoke of a place called Tophet, which was a place in the Valley of Hinnom.

> "For Tophet was established of old,
> Yes, for the king it is prepared.
> He has made it deep and large;
> Its pyre is fire with much wood;
> The breath of the LORD, like a stream
> of brimstone,
> Kindles it" (Isaiah 30:33).

According to Isaiah, Tophet, or the Valley of Hinnom, was established in ancient times, and the Lord is the One who made it deep and large and who stokes the flames of hell with His breath. Scripture further identifies the geographic location of Tophet in regards to ancient Jerusalem. "Thus saith the LORD, Go and get a potter's earthen bottle, and take of the ancients of the people, and of the ancients of the priests; And go forth unto the valley of the son of Hinnom, which is by the entry of the east gate, and proclaim there the words that I shall tell thee" (Jeremiah 19:1-2 KJV).

The Valley of the Son of Hinnom was accessed through the east gate of the original walls around Jerusalem, and the modern day location is the valley that connects the Valley of Jehoshaphat and the Kidron Valley. This same place where the Israelites sacrificed their children in the fire to Molech later became a garbage dump where refuse, dead carcasses, executed bodies and human waste were burned during Jesus' time. Jesus referred figuratively to this burning garbage dump outside of Jerusalem as "hell" or *Gehenna* eleven times in Scripture. *Gehenna* is not a Greek word, but a phonetic transcription of Aramaic *Gehenna* that referred to the Valley of the Son of Hinnom. Jesus used the word *Gehenna* to describe this physical place outside the city walls of Jerusalem as a place of everlasting punishment.

The Lord revealed to me there was a gate to hell that was located in the same place He called Gehenna in the Valley of Hinnom. Scriptures verify there are gates or portals to hell. "Have the gates of death been revealed to you? Or have you seen the doors of the shadow of death? (Job 38:17). "In the prime of my life I shall go to the gates of Sheol; I am deprived of the remainder of my years" (Isaiah 38:10).

In fact, the Lord said to me: ***"Child, there are gates of hell. One of the gates of hell is in Jerusalem in the Valley of Hinnom. The gates open and demons come from hell with their assignments. Demons also return through the gate to report back. I will show you this phenomenon in the spirit when you are in Israel."***

While I was in Israel, this is the vision the Holy Spirit showed me. I saw a large black-winged demon with huge, claw-like feet flying through the air. He had a man in his claws and was flying towards an ancient wooden gate on the ground. The archaic gate, which was very weathered, was constructed of thick wooden planks held together with large, primitive iron spikes. When the demon flew over the gate with the man's body, the gate swung open from the ground to reveal a dark opening. This demon had the power to open the gate just by hovering above it! When the demon dropped the man's body into the dark abyss, the gates closed.

Then I saw a scene in this vision that caused me to gasp. There were such a massive number of people being brought to this opening by a multitude of demons that the gate did not have a chance to shut before the next person was brought and dropped in. There was a veritable procession of demons flying through the air, bringing these condemned people to this gate of hell. The Spirit of God revealed to me that these condemned people entered hell through this gate and traveled down a funnel-like passageway until they reached their destination in hell. He said they will be punished in hell until the thousand-year reign of Christ on earth has been completed. Right after the thousand-year reign of Christ on earth, all the dead will stand before Him and be judged. The righteous will be judged separately at the Bema seat of Christ and receive their rewards. "For we must all appear before the judgment seat of Christ, that each one may receive the things done in the body, according to what he has done, whether good or bad" (2 Corinthians 5:10).

The unrighteous will be judged at the Great White Throne Judgment seat.

> "Then I saw a great white throne and Him who sat on it, from whose face the earth and the heaven fled away. And there was found no place for them. And I saw the dead, small and great, standing before God, and books were opened. And another book was opened, which is the Book of Life. And the dead were judged according to their works, by the things which were written in the books. The sea gave up the dead who were in it, and Death and Hades delivered up the dead who were in them. And they were judged, each one according to his works. Then Death and Hades were cast into the lake of fire. This is the second death. And anyone not found written in the Book of Life was cast into the lake of fire" (Revelation 20:11-15).

People will be resurrected and standing alive before Christ at both of these judgment seats. But before the Bema seat of Christ and Great White Throne judgment, there will be another resurrection. This first resurrection of the dead will be only for the righteous that have been martyred for the Name of Jesus Christ, and they will reign with Jesus during the thousand years.

> "And I saw thrones, and they sat on them, and judgment was committed to them. Then I saw the souls of those who had been beheaded for their witness to Jesus and for the word of God, who had not worshiped the beast or his image, and had not received his mark on their foreheads or on their hands. And they lived and reigned with Christ for a thousand years. But the rest of the dead did not live again until the thousand years were finished. This is the first resurrection. Blessed and holy is he who has part in the first resurrection. Over such the second death has no power, but they shall be priests of God and of Christ, and shall reign with Him a thousand years" (Revelation 20:4-6).

The second resurrection will occur when all the unrighteous and righteous are raised from the dead to stand before Christ and be judged, at either the Bema or the Great White Throne Judgment Seat. Scripture also states there is a second death. The righteous will not experience the second death after being resurrected, but the unrighteous will experience this second death. "He who has an ear, let him hear what the Spirit says to the churches. He who overcomes shall not be hurt by the second death" (Revelation 2:11). "But the cowardly, unbelieving, abominable, murderers, sexually immoral, sorcerers, idolaters, and all liars shall have their part in the lake which burns with fire and brimstone, which is the second death" (Revelation 21:8). The second death is being thrown alive into the lake of fire! The flaming fires of hell are real for those who have been condemned to the second death due to their refusal to accept Jesus as their Savior.

The Holy Spirit also showed me a second gate to hell. When I was in the northern part of Israel, I visited a place in Caesarea Philippi where the ancient temple of Pan was located during the days of Jesus. On the side of this stone precipice was a large cave or grotto that once contained a natural spring. The Temple of Pan was built directly in front of this grotto and spring. The people who worshipped Pan would take their first-born children and offer them to Pan by throwing the live babies into the spring. If a baby died, then Pan accepted their sacrifice. If the newborn survived or there was any blood in the waters running from the spring, then the sacrifice was not accepted by Pan. This was the same location in Caesarea Philippi where Jesus was with His disciples and spoke these words:

> "When Jesus came into the region of Caesarea Philippi, He asked His disciples, saying, 'Who do men say that I, the Son of Man, am?' So they said, 'Some *say* John the Baptist, some Elijah, and others Jeremiah or one of the prophets.' He said to them, 'But who do you say that I am?' Simon Peter answered and said, 'You are the Christ, the Son of the living God.' Jesus answered and said to him, 'Blessed are you,

Simon Bar-Jonah, for flesh and blood has not revealed *this* to you, but My Father who is in heaven. And I also say to you that you are Peter, and on this rock I will build My church, and the gates of Hades shall not prevail against it. And I will give you the keys of the kingdom of heaven, and whatever you bind on earth will be bound in heaven, and whatever you loose on earth will be loosed in heaven.' Then He commanded His disciples that they should tell no one that He was Jesus the Christ" (Matthew 16:13-20).

The gates of Hades that Jesus was referring to were this grotto and temple where they were sacrificing babies to Pan. Today, it is still a grotto, and the Spirit of God revealed to me that this location is another gate to hell where the demons take people who have been condemned to hell. When I was in Israel and stood looking at this grotto, I could feel the presence of evil like an oppressive force slamming into my chest. When a spirit-filled child of God infiltrates the enemy's territory, the demons will make their presence known to drive away the presence of Christ. This has been an established gate to hell for eons, and the demons manifested their presence to let me know this was their turf. The Lord showed me these two gates to hell so I could warn people about the impending judgment that awaits them if they continue to refuse Jesus Christ's forgiveness for their sins.

~ CHAPTER TWO ~

Location of Hell

I was praying in tongues and was in the Spirit, and the Lord said to me: *"I want to show you parts of hell."* This is what I saw and sensed as I began to travel in the Spirit downward through an earthen tunnel. I was not free falling down this vertical tunnel; it was a controlled descent. There was a wall all around me, and there was a musty damp smell. The walls of this passageway changed to different layers of rock, and as the rock changed, I knew I was traveling deeper into the earth. When the rocks began to seep water, I instinctively knew I was passing through a water table.

The tunnel became black and there was a putrid smell. I sensed I was traveling through a layer of coal and natural gas. Next, the wall of the tunnel was lined with dark brown, ancient looking rocks with variegated pieces. Finally, the wall of the tunnel was a black, shiny rock. The temperature rose as I descended, and I heard screams from a distance. I could still feel something pulling me down this vertical tunnel, and when I tried to yank my foot away, the grip got tighter.

My descent ended, and I was standing in a small, dark earthen cave-like room that smelled of mold. I noticed that there were three openings in this cave, and I heard a voice saying, "Which way shall we take her?" Then another voice said, "Take her to the left. I want her to see the punishment that awaits those in hell." I sensed the voice was demonic and his statement was meant to frighten me, but I was not afraid because I knew I was a child of God, and my eternal destination is in heaven. I was taken to the left opening, and I saw people chained to earthen walls, and they were crying out, "Please help us. We have been here a long time." Then I saw metal bars similar to those of a jail cell, and people stood behind the bars. Their faces looked old, and there was weariness in their eyes unlike anything I had ever seen before. I saw a large rat gnawing at the foot of a woman in a jail cell. She kicked at the rat until she was so exhausted from defending herself that she permitted the rat to eat her flesh. Then the rat transformed into a demon, and it tormented this woman with a hideous mocking laugh.

I saw large snakes slithering in and out of holes in these earthen jail cells, and they also tortured people with their presence. Several months after God showed me this part of hell, my college-aged daughter approached me about a very disturbing dream she had. I had not revealed to her the visions the Lord had shown me about hell. When she explained her dream, I was in awe how perfectly she described what I had already witnessed in hell. The Lord gave my daughter a spiritual dream of hell as confirmation that what He had shown me was real because two is also the number of witness in scripture!

In the dream, my daughter descended down a set of stairs to a place under the earth, and she knew it was hell. She saw thick round bars made of metal that were embedded in a reddish colored rock. Behind this set of disgusting bars was a small cave- like jail cell that was repulsive. Inside the jail cell she saw two rats and a pile of human bones. One rat was half eaten, and she could see the exposed ribs of the rat. The other rat was alive and sitting by the human bones. The Holy Spirit revealed to her that the rats had eaten all the flesh from the body of the human, and this torture in hell was not a one-time event. The flesh of this person would be restored, and the rat would eat the person again and again. The Spirit of God also revealed to her that being ravished by rats was one of the lower forms of punishment of hell and this was just the beginning of the torture. When she turned to leave this horrific scene, she saw a long passageway with many similar jail cells embedded in the earth. There were arms and hands reaching out of these cells, and she described the color of their flesh as a bloated, pasty white, almost as if their bodies had been dead in water for several days.

She was full of fear about viewing anything else in hell, so she ran up the stairs as rats nipped at her feet. Her dream of hell and my vision of hell matched exactly in detail. We both descended downwards into hell. We both saw the rats eating the flesh of people in jail cells that looked like caves with iron bars. We both witnessed the many jail cells that lined this long corridor of damp, dark stone. The Lord revealed this part of hell to both me and my daughter as a testimony that hell is a place with horrific punishment.

The Lord gave me further details about my spiritual experience of traveling to hell and the horrors He showed me in the spirit: *"There is a funnel like whirlwind over the gates of hell that the demons drop the condemned. Once they are in this funnel, they are on their way to hell. The same shaft you traveled down in the spirit is the same one the condemned souls travel to hell. Once they reach the room you were in, they are assigned to a part of hell depending on their sin. There are various punishments for various sins. There is a section of hell for unbelievers, for the sexually immoral, for the murderers, for Satan worshippers, for the false teachers who lead My sheep astray, and for others. Each one will receive their punishment according to their sin. The only sin on earth that is unforgiveable is the sin of unbelief in My Son Jesus Christ. All other sins are pardonable if they repent and put their faith and trust in Jesus."* God desires to spare people from the torments of hell, but scripture sternly warns sinners that without Christ, they will go to hell.

> "For if God did not spare angels when they sinned, but sent them to hell, putting them in chains of darkness to be held for judgment; if he did not spare the ancient world when he brought the flood on its ungodly people, but protected Noah, a preacher of righteousness, and seven others; if he condemned the cities of Sodom and Gomorrah by burning them to ashes, and made them an example of what is going to happen to the ungodly; and if he rescued Lot, a righteous man, who was distressed by the depraved conduct of the lawless (for that righteous man, living among

them day after day, was tormented in his righteous soul by the lawless deeds he saw and heard) — if this is so, then the Lord knows how to rescue the godly from trials and to hold the unrighteous for punishment on the day of judgment" (2 Peter 2:4-9).

After I had this vision of hell, I pondered about the different levels of the earth I had traveled through before I reached this section of hell. My scientific mind begged to know where I was during this spiritual experience. I researched the various layers of the earth and was amazed that what I saw as I descended matched exactly with geologic findings of the layers of the earth.

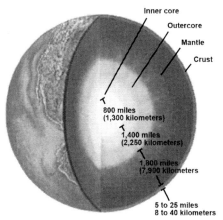

There are several layers of the earth, and each layer has a different composition, mass, and depth. These layers consist of the earth's crust, the upper and lower mantle, the outer core and the inner core. I traveled through the earth's crust which is about twenty-five miles of brown earth, different layers of rocks, the water tables, and the coal and natural gas.

1   http://upload.wikimedia.org/wikipedia/en/1/1b/Earth_layers_NASA.png

Next I traveled through the upper mantle of the variegated rock which was the quartz. The lower mantle of the earth was the shiny black rock which was the basaltic layer. Basalt is a molten rock similar to lava that is formed and then hardened when the mantle of the earth becomes compressed.

From what the Spirit has shown me and science confirms, hell begins in the lower mantle of the earth. Scripture verifies that hell is located in the lower parts of the earth. "There *is* Elam and all her multitude, All around her grave, All of them slain, fallen by the sword, Who have gone down uncircumcised to the lower parts of the earth, Who caused their terror in the land of the living; Now they bear their shame with those who go down to the Pit" (Ezekiel 32:24). Scripture also states that after the Great White Throne Judgment of Christ, anyone whose name is not written in the Book of Life will be thrown into the lake of fire. Although the center of the earth's inner core is extremely hot and solid; the outer core of the earth is a fiery hot molten mass of metal that matches the description of the lake of fire. The graphic illustration shows that the location of hell is in the lower parts of the earth which is the earth's mantle, and the location of the lake of fire is in the earth's outer core. My scientific mind was satisfied that the place I traveled in the Spirit completely matched the geologic makeup of the earth's layers. Science and Spirit will always coincide because God is the creator of the heavens, the earth, and all that is below the earth.

CHAPTER THREE

Belly of Hell

I was worshipping the Lord and praying in the Spirit when the Lord said: *"I want to show you another part of hell called the Belly of Hell. This is the largest part of hell, and people are tortured day and night. This is where the murderers, the rapists, the homosexuals, the adulterers, the pedophiles, the drug traffickers and the like go. According to their transgression, they are punished. These are Satan's children, and he determines how they are punished. Their fate is in his hands, and he is cruel punisher. In this part of hell, the demons torture those souls according to the command of Satan. These people will be tortured until the Great White Throne Judgment whereby they will be judged by God and then thrown into the lake of fire where the fire is never quenched.*

There are ancients in hell that have been tortured for thousands of years, and more are added to hell every day. The demons and Satan can travel freely from hell to earth until God's final Day of Judgment. Even those who worshipped Satan on earth and had great demonic power cannot return to earth once they are dead. Satan promises greater power and position to those who serve him, but this is a great deception because these people are chained in everlasting prisons in hell. I want to show you how some people are tortured so you can warn people of the consequences of sin."

These are three visions the Lord showed me in the Spirit regarding the torture that occurs in hell. In the first vision, I watched with utter astonishment at the movements and the outward appearance of this small demon with an oversized mouth. It had many jagged teeth protruding from his mouth and extremely large ears compared to his small body. It had skinny straight legs, claw-like hands and feet, and a rat-like tail. A command was given to this demon to bite a person who was in a jail cell in hell. It hopped up and down with glee on its chicken like legs and cackled a high-pitched revolting laugh because it delighted at the prospect of torturing this person. I could not fathom this kind of merriment and excitement about inflicting agony, but these demons are sadistic in nature, and their blackened hearts only know hate and cruelty. This demon flew through the air and latched onto a man's shoulder and sank its teeth into his flesh. The man screamed as another demon did the same thing and sank its teeth into another part of his body. Several demons did this until the man sank to the ground in agony because of the excruciating pain.

The next thing I witnessed in the Spirit was a multitude of people chained together by leg irons. They were being led in a long procession like convicts chained together. The line was so extensive; I could not see the end. These people were hopeless and devoid of any facial expression, almost like zombies. They entered a large arena, and when it was full,

Satan came to the center of the stadium. The people were forced to bow down and worship him, and it seemed like their worship empowered Satan. While their worship was in full adulation, Satan twirled around with one swift movement like a tornado. Satan's violent cyclone was transformed into a massive flaming inferno that burned everyone's flesh in the stadium. All the people were in excruciating agony from the flames that scorched their flesh, and they screamed and fell down. The group of flesh-seared people was led away as a new crowd waited to enter the stadium. The same ritual and torture was exacted upon the next group. I sensed everyone in hell would be subjected to this flaming torture, and they all would be required to worship Satan.

The third form of torture I saw in the Spirit was a man lying on a stone slab. He was chained to it so he could not escape. The room was empty except this man on the slab, and he was anxiously waiting for what was about to come. Part of his torment was waiting for his painful ordeal to begin. As he waited with dread, there was anguish written on his face. Finally, a large, hairy ape like demon came into the room wielding a large sword. He approached the man and began to swing the sword in the air to place fear and trepidation in the man. The man began to groan. He knew what was coming because he had already been tortured like this a thousand times before. The large, hairy demon lifted the sword above the man's chest and then plunged the sword into the man's heart. Blood flowed from his heart, and his eyes rolled back in his head. I could see and sense the agony in this condemned man, and the Lord said, *"There are many forms of torture in the belly of hell, and I have given you glimpses of three.*

Warn people so they do not have to suffer the terrors of hell."

There are biblical references to the belly of hell called the belly of Sheol and the heart of the earth. "Then Jonah prayed to the LORD his God from the fish's belly. And he said: 'I cried out to the LORD because of my affliction, And He answered me. Out of the belly of Sheol I cried, And you answered my voice'" (Jonah 2:1-2). "For as Jonah was three days and three nights in the belly of the great fish, so will the Son of Man be three days and three nights in the heart of the earth" (Matthew 12:40). Jesus was in the heart of the earth before He rose from the dead because He had a mission to fulfill. "Now this, 'He ascended'—what does it mean but that He also first descended into the lower parts of the earth?" (Ephesians 4:9).

When Jesus descended into the lower parts, He admonished the demonic spirits that He had the victory over sin and Satan. He did not preach a salvation message because it was too late for those already in hell. Jesus made it known to these rebellious spirits that He was the Christ, and He would not remain in Sheol because He would rise from the dead on the third day. "For Christ also suffered once for sins, the just for the unjust, that He might bring us to God, being put to death in the flesh but made alive by the Spirit, by whom also He went and preached to the spirits in prison, who formerly were disobedient" (1 Peter 3:18-20). Those in hell do not get a second chance, but those on earth do! We have the privilege of living on this side of the finished work of the cross. Jesus Christ has already paid the price for our sins so we do not have to endure the torments of hell.

~ CHAPTER FOUR ~

Legs of Hell

God's desire is that no one perishes in hell, yet He will not remove man's freedom of choice to accomplish His desire. Decisions that are made on earth directly affect one's eternal destination along with rewards in heaven or punishment in hell. My journey into another section of hell began while I was worshipping the Lord and praying in the Spirit. The Holy Spirit beckoned me to a verse of scripture in the book of Isaiah to encourage me to declare what I was about to view in this other part of hell. "For thus has the Lord said to me: 'Go, set a watchman; let him declare what he sees'" (Isaiah 21:6). Then the Lord spoke these words to me right before I descended in the Spirit into another part of hell: *"I will show you the Legs of Hell. Do not fear, for I am with you. You are My prophet, child. Declare what I show you. What you will view will stun you and cause you great anguish."*

My spiritual journey began when I was in a very long horizontal earthen tunnel. It was very dark, but I knew it was in hell. Then suddenly, there was a bright flash of light that lit up a wall in this tunnel. There I saw bars of a jail cell embedded in the earthen wall that was made of a very hard stone. In this small cave like cell there was an old woman with long grey hair sitting in a chair. Her face was wrinkled, and her eyes were recessed in the hollows of her weathered face.

She was rocking back and forth, and when she noticed I was there, she stood and gripped the bars of the cell. She said, "Let me tell you my story." I was hesitant and wanted to retreat, but the Spirit of the Lord told me to permit her to tell her story. She began to unfold her story to me. "Once, I was a beautiful woman. Men were attracted to me, and I took advantage of my beauty. I led many men astray with my charm and my voluptuous body. I slept with many married men and high officials in the land. I was paid well and lived a life of luxury. When my beauty began to fade, I became a madam of many beautiful young women. I sold them into a life of prostitution, of which many never escaped. I am here because of my life of prostitution, and I am forever bound to this cell because I led many women into the same life. While I was on earth, I refused to listen to the ones God sent to me. I have been in this cell all alone day after day for many years. I placed much value on my outward appearance and my ability to lure men, but now my beauty has faded, and I will be an old wrinkled woman for all eternity bound to this cell. Tell women that a life of prostitution and adultery will ensure them a place in hell just like this jail cell. I endure many forms of torture, and it never ends. Hell is a real place with suffering and torment."

I felt the hand of an angel moving me further along this tunnel, and I could hear the hopeless heart wrenching cries of people screaming, "Get me out of here! I repent of my sin!" We stopped at another jail cell, and once again, the cell was lit up so I could see inside. There was a vile looking man who had pointy ears, fang like teeth, and his eyes were lifeless black orbs. He screamed, "I have power!" The Spirit of God revealed to me he was once a warlock highly elevated in the satanic realm. This man began to rapidly morph into a rat, then a snake, then a cat, and finally back to a man. This constant swift morphing was a bitter reminder of the power he once possessed on earth through Satan, but now he was confined to prison as an impotent man that had no control over his body. This was part of his punishment in hell for selling his soul to Satan. He believed Satan would give him great power and position, but instead, he was confined to this small jail cell powerless to stop his body from transforming into animals.

We moved further down the passageway of this Leg of Hell, and this time I was shocked to see a teenage boy chained to a wall with a leg iron. He had a pick ax in his hands, and he was digging like a coal miner into the hard rock. The Holy Spirit revealed to me that part of his punishment in hell was to dig more cells in the Legs of Hell. It was difficult labor because the rock was very hard, and it was emotionally tormenting because he knew he was making a cell for another person to be held captive. The sweat was rolling down his brow, and when he turned to me there were tears in his eyes. He said to me, "I am here because I was rebellious to my parents. One night I went with my friends and we all got drunk. On the way home we were in a car accident and I was killed. When I woke from the nightmare of the car accident, I was here. I regret that night every day I am in hell. My parents told me about Jesus, but I would not listen. I will never see them again, and I cry every day. I miss my mom and my dad."

When this young man told me his story I began to weep uncontrollably. I wanted to wrap my arms around him and tell him everything was going to be alright, but I knew he was here for eternity, and my heart was wrenching. The tears, heaviness and sorrow I felt was so overwhelming that the Spirit of Lord had to comfort me before I could move further down this leg of Hell.

We journeyed deep into this cavernous section of hell, and for the fourth time I was standing in front of a set of bars. The cell lit up to show a man standing in the center of the cell with a saber in his hand. He swung the saber in a circular motion that was impressive. By his adept use of the sword, I knew he was well trained in using this weapon. The Holy Spirit revealed to me that he was a mass murderer. He had killed many of his countrymen by the edge of the sword in an attempt to eradicate a certain ethnic group of people. The Spirit revealed to me he was responsible for the genocide attempt of a people group in an African nation. I pondered in my heart if he was a part of the massacre of the Tutsi by the Hutu in Rwanda in 1994. As I watched this man expertly carve the sword through the air, I was shocked by what he did next. He plunged the sword into his own heart and fell onto the ground as his blood profusely spilled over the earthen floor of his cell. The Spirit of God revealed to me this was his punishment in hell for killing so many by the sword. He would plunge the saber into his own heart, and he felt the excruciating pain every time he repeated this tortuous, masochistic act.

The next dungeon cubicle held captive two female prisoners. When the jail cell was illuminated and they saw me, they both pressed up against the bars and beckoned me to come closer. One of the women reached out and grabbed my arm and pleaded with me to listen to their story. "My name is Rachael and this is my partner Nina. We were lesbian lovers in New Hampshire, and we were instrumental in the passage of laws to permit same sex marriages. We were proponents of the gay movement that quickly took root in the USA. We are here in hell because of our lesbian lives and our involvement in legalizing homosexuality. The religious activists that battled against us warned us about the sin of homosexuality, but we would not listen. We were so in love with each other, and we wanted everyone to have the opportunity to openly express their love for their same sex mates. The intense love we had for each other was so strong that it seemed to overtake us at times. After arriving in hell, we learned that we were deceived because this strong love we had for each other was actually a spirit of lust. This type of lustful love is forbidden by God. We sit in this barren cell and stare at each other as a constant reminder of our wicked way of life and how we led others down the same path and to the same place in hell. We were deceived. Nina and I vowed we would spend eternity together, but to our horror, that eternity is in hell."

"Child, I want to show you another Leg of Hell." I asked the Lord to prepare my heart because these visions were very graphic and emotionally taxing. The Lord strengthened me before He showed me the shocking forms of punishments in a second Leg of Hell. The first thing I viewed was a man chained to an earthen wall. His hands were chained above his head, and his back was bare. I saw a whip slice across his back and rip open his flesh. He was thrashed until his back looked like a piece of raw, bloody meat. He slumped against the wall, but his chained hands prevented him from falling to the ground. I moved along this earthen corridor, and I could hear groans of agony and smell the putrid scent of burning flesh. I observed a long procession of people standing in a line in this passageway.

When I arrived at this room of torture, the screams got louder. I saw a demon with a long metal pole. At the end of the pole was a five pointed star surrounded by a circle. The demon placed this pole into a scorching fire until the star was glowing red. Then this red hot metal star was branded onto the right shoulder of each person. When the searing metal brand came in contact with the skin, horrifying screams followed. I could hear the sizzle of the seared skin, and I could smell the stench of the burning flesh. The smell of burnt flesh and the heavy smoke that permeated this hellhole of torment was nauseating. The Spirit of the Lord told me this brand was marking each person in hell as a child of Satan.

The cave like room I was escorted to next was ghastly beyond comprehension, and it will be forever etched into my mind. I saw a vile looking demon holding a wooden stake in one hand and a crude metal mallet in the other. The demon was grinning so I could see his razor sharp teeth. His breath smelled like an open septic tank. This demon walked over to an earthen wall, and what I observed caused me to groan out loud. There were people attached to the wall with wooden stakes pierced though their body. Some people had stakes driven between their eyes that pinned their head to the wall. Some had stakes through their heart or their mid section and some through their hands. The entire wall was plastered with these lifeless bodies that had been staked to it as a ritualistic torturous act. In this same vision I saw a man screaming while this depraved demon forcibly drug him to this wall of hell. The man began to spit on the demon, but it just mockingly snorted out a revolting laugh. The demon shoved the wooden stake in the man's mouth, shoved him against the wall, and hammered the stake until it protruded through the back of his neck and pinned him to the wall. I was completely appalled and sickened by what I had witnessed.

The last scene I viewed in this Leg of Hell was also very disturbing. In a large earthen room, there was an elevated wooden platform that was accessed by a set of steps. Above this platform, attached to the stone ceiling was a row of nooses. Once again I saw a line of people waiting to climb the set of stairs leading to this wooden platform. The nooses were placed around their necks, and then all of a sudden, the wooden floor swung down and they were dangling from the ceiling by the nooses. After a few minutes the nooses were mysteriously released from their necks, and the people dropped into a large, deep pit below. I could see the pit was filled with a multitude of bodies. The next group of people would ascend the steps to the platform, and the same torture was meted out.

While journeying in this Leg of Hell, the Holy Spirit explained about the physical shape of hell. He said: ***"The Belly of Hell is the center and the largest part of hell. The Legs of Hell are smaller sections that fork out from the center. There are four Legs of Hell that extend from the belly in four directions. Each of the Legs of Hell contains people who have grievously sinned against My commandments. Repent, for the kingdom of God is at hand. Hell is a real place. Hell is a place for all those who refuse to obey My commandments,*** *will not repent of their sin, and reject salvation through Jesus Christ."*

God has given us His commandments in the Bible to follow, so we must have knowledge of them. Ignorance is no excuse; neither is the errant teaching that states because we are under grace, we are not required to follow the Ten Commandments. Jesus said, "If you love Me, keep My commandments" (John 14:15).

The Ten Commandments (Exodus 20:1-17):
1. **You shall have no other gods before Me.**
2. **You shall not make for yourself a carved image.**
3. **You shall not take the name of the LORD your God in vain, for the LORD will not hold him guiltless who takes His name in vain.**
4. **Remember the Sabbath day, to keep it holy. Six days you shall labor and do all your work, but the seventh day is the Sabbath of the LORD your God.**
5. **Honor your father and your mother, that your days may be long upon the land which the LORD your God is giving you.**
6. **You shall not murder.**
7. **You shall not commit adultery.**
8. **You shall not steal.**
9. **You shall not bear false witness against your neighbor.**
10. **You shall not covet your neighbor's house; you shall not covet your neighbor's wife.**

After my visions of the Legs of Hell, I knew I was shown

these particular people in hell and their specific punishments so I could declare what I witnessed. My heart was wrenching, and my spirit was heavy because I knew these people would be there for eternity, and there was nothing I could do to alleviate their anguish. The Spirit of the Lord reminded that He had shown me these visions so that many can be saved from this everlasting torment. Although I cannot change the eternal destination of those I saw in hell, I can be God's mouthpiece to herald His truth so that others can get saved from this eternal torture.

~ Chapter Five ~

Bottomless Pit

There is a partition in hell called the Bottomless Pit, where Satan is king. "And they had as king over them the angel of the bottomless pit, whose name in Hebrew is Abaddon, but in Greek he has the name Apollyon" (Revelation 9:11). Abaddon and Apollyon is a reference to Satan, and it means "the destroyer." There are demons that have been locked in the Bottomless Pit by an angel of the Lord, and they will be released to harm Satan's children during the last three and a half years of Tribulation on earth. Even though the Bottomless Pit is Satan's domain, God's sovereignty still reigns above Satan's complete control of it. This is demonstrated by the fact that these demons are held captive and only the angel in heaven can release them. Once they are released, these demons have limited power because they are not permitted to harm any person that has the seal of God on their forehead.

God will send two witnesses to the earth during the first three and a half years of the Tribulation, and no one will have the power to kill them. These two witnesses will be Enoch and Elijah; the two people in scripture that were taken to heaven but did not experience death. Anyone who tries to kill them will be destroyed by fire that proceeds from their mouths. The demons will not be able to able to destroy them either, so Satan will come up from the bottomless pit to kill them.

> "When they finish their testimony, the beast that ascends out of the bottomless pit will make war against them, overcome them, and kill them. And their dead bodies will lie in the street of the great city which spiritually is called Sodom and Egypt, where also our Lord was crucified. Then those from the peoples, tribes, tongues, and nations will see their dead bodies three and a half days, and not allow their dead bodies to be put into graves. And those who dwell on the earth will rejoice over them, make merry, and send gifts to one another because these two prophets tormented those who dwell on the earth" (Revelation 11:7-10).

The Bottomless Pit could be considered Satan's "headquarters," where his planning and scheming takes place. I saw a vision of one of the rooms in the Bottomless Pit where Satan operates. I noticed a big, round granite table. Patterned in the middle of the marble was a five-pointed star surrounded by a circle. There was an ornate, gold candelabrum that had six receptacles, but there were no candles or any place for oil. A demon pointed at the candelabra, and the flames came out of the receptacles. This meeting room was extremely ornate. Fashioned into the walls were golden gargoyle images; the demonic-looking creatures had red gemstones for eyes that eerily glowed. This vision was like a clip from a movie, and as it began to unfold, a meeting was about to commence. There were several high-ranking demons chattering when Satan entered the room. Satan wore a cape that draped to the floor. The demons also had on various uniforms that looked like military uniforms emblazoned with various medallions. Each demon wore a different uniform that represented the nations that he had dominion over. It was a very formal affair.

Satan took his seat at the table in an ornately decorated and gem studded chair. One-by-one, the demons gave their report on the different areas of the world. New strategies were planned, but if the old strategies were still working, they remained in place. At the end of the meeting, I saw a goblet in front of each of the demon generals. They took an oath to Satan and sealed the oath by drinking human blood from their goblets.

The Lord spoke these words to me regarding the battle and strategy of the spiritual realm: *"In your army, there are generals, colonels, captains, sergeants, and privates. Most often it is the privates, sergeants, and captains that go into battle, while the generals and the colonels plan the strategy. But when the battle gets fierce, the colonels and the generals are on the battlefield. It is the same in the spiritual realm. The demons of lower rank are the ones battling the angels of lower rank. When there is a high-ranking demon that comes against the lower ranking angel, then I must send a stronger higher-ranking angel to do battle. I sent Daniel an angel, but he was detained for twenty-one days by a higher-ranking prince of darkness; the prince of Persia. Michael who is also a high-ranking prince came and fought with the prince of Persia so the other angel could go to Daniel. The strongest and most powerful Archangels are princes over a region or nation. They are warriors and fighters. Michael is the prince over Israel. There are also fallen angels that are princes over entire regions and nations. The prince of Persia and the prince of Greece are principalities."*

> "Then he said to me, 'Do not fear, Daniel, for from the first day that you set your heart to understand, and to humble yourself before your God, your words were heard; and I have come because of your words. But the prince of the kingdom of Persia withstood me twenty-one days; and behold, Michael, one of the chief princes, came to help me, for I had been left alone there with the kings of Persia. Now I have come to make you understand what will happen to your people in the latter days, for the vision refers to many days yet to come'" (Daniel 10:12-14).

Another reference to the hierarchy of the demonic realm is found in Ephesians. "Put on the whole armor of God, that you may be able to stand against the wiles of the devil. For we do not wrestle against flesh and blood, but against principalities, against powers, against the rulers of the darkness of this age, against spiritual hosts of wickedness in the heavenly places" (Ephesians 6:11-13). God's irony and justice will see that Satan is bound in chains in his own headquarters for one thousand years during the millennial reign of Jesus Christ on earth. During Christ's reign on earth, Satan will not be able to deceive people.

> "Then I saw an angel coming down from heaven, having the key to the bottomless pit and a great chain in his hand. He laid hold of the dragon, that serpent of old, who is the Devil and Satan, and bound him for a thousand years; and he cast him into the bottomless pit, and shut him up, and set a seal on him, so that he should deceive the nations no more till the thousand years were finished. But after these things he must be released for a little while" (Revelation 20:1-4).

During the Millennial reign of Christ, there will be people on earth who rebel against Jesus. After the thousand years are over, Satan will be released from the Bottomless Pit by an angel of the Lord so he can gather all the rebellious people of the earth for the final battle of God and Magog.

> "Now when the thousand years have expired, Satan will be released from his prison and will go out to deceive the nations which are in the four corners of the earth, Gog and Magog, to gather them together to battle, whose number is as the sand of the sea. They went up on the breadth of the earth and surrounded the camp of the saints and the beloved city. And fire came down from God out of heaven and devoured them" (Revelation 20:7-9).

You would think that after experiencing the chains

of bondage for one thousand years that Satan would admit defeat, but he does not. Pride and hatred will keep Satan forging ahead under the delusion that he can conquer Jesus. He will gather the rebellious nations together and convince them he can overpower Jesus, but the Father in heaven will destroy the armies with fire. Then Satan will be finally cast into the Lake of fire which will be his final place of torture for all eternity. He will be in the exact same place that all the sinful people he tortured in the Belly of Hell and the Legs of Hell. They will look at Satan and rejoice that he has been brought down to their level, which will be the most devastating form of torture Satan will have to endure for eternity.

~ CHAPTER SIX ~

Lake of Fire

The Lake of Fire is the final destination of Satan, all the demons, the Antichrist, the false prophet and all sinners after the Great White Throne Judgment of God.

> "The devil, who deceived them, was cast into the lake of fire and brimstone where the beast and the false prophet are. And they will be tormented day and night forever and ever. Then I saw a great white throne and Him who sat on it, from whose face the earth and the heaven fled away. And there was found no place for them. And I saw the dead, small and great, standing before God, and books were opened. And another book was opened, which is the Book of Life. And the dead were judged according to their works, by the things which were written in the books. The sea gave up the dead who were in it, and Death and Hades delivered up the dead who were in them. And they were judged, each one according to his

works. Then Death and Hades were cast into the lake of fire. This is the second death. And anyone not found written in the Book of Life was cast into the lake of fire" (Revelation 20: 10-15).

The Lord gave me a glimpse of the Lake of Fire in a vision. The first thing I saw was an earthen cliff. I was at the edge of this high cliff looking down, and I could see a glowing, red lake beneath. It was a bubbling, hot mass of liquid that was blazing and a visible vapor danced over the scarlet waves. Then I witnessed a gavel slamming down on a table, and I heard a loud voice announce, "Adulterer."

The next thing I witnessed shocked me. I saw a man being thrown over the cliff into this red, glowing lake. He let out an ear piercing scream as he tumbled a great distance toward the pit. His body hit the red-hot liquid, and his flesh was instantly burnt off. Again, I heard the gavel slam, and an authoritative voice said, "Liar; thief," and more people were being cast into the Lake of Fire. There were so many bodies in this massive pool of molten liquid that they were getting entangled with each other. The scene was horrible, almost surreal.

Then the Holy Spirit spoke these words to me: ***"The Lake of Fire is located in the center of the earth, and it is the final destination for all who are condemned. Satan will be cast into the Lake of Fire just as the Anti-Christ and false prophet will. The Anti-Christ and the false prophet will not get a chance to stand before God at the Great White Throne Judgment because they will be cast alive*** *into the Lake of Fire and will remain there for all eternity.*

The torments of the Lake of Fire never end. All those who have died without Christ's forgiveness are in different parts of hell until they are found guilty at the Great White Throne Judgment. Dead men cannot stand before God to receive their judgment. They will be resurrected and have a body when they receive their sentence, and that is why it is called the second death. When they are cast alive into the Lake of Fire, the body experiences a horrific death. They will remain in the Lake of Fire for all eternity. Imagine being trapped in a prison without any hope of ever gaining your freedom while knowing that the torture will never end. The soul is hopeless in the Lake of Fire, and the spirit becomes broken and desperate. The desperation never ends. Imagine thinking to yourself, while you are in prison, all of the ways you could have prevented the situation you are in. Some people will constantly regret the sin that placed them there, and they will regret refusing Jesus' forgiveness for their sin.

The mental anguish will be overwhelming, and they will weep, but to no avail. Those that were not repentant of their sin and did not regret refusing Jesus, will gnash their teeth in anger. The anger and hatred will consume their souls. They will never admit that their sin has placed them in the Lake of Fire, and their mental anguish will be worse because they believe they are being unjustly punished by God. The Lake of Fire will truly be an eternal prison for the body, soul and the spirit of the condemned. They will feel the flames for all eternity. They will feel their flesh being burnt by the flames, smell the stench of their burning bodies, and hear their own screams of agony. This will be a continuous punishment that never ends. I know it is difficult to understand how a person can experience death over and over again, but this is what happens in hell. Hell is a horrible place to go! Tell them so they will repent of their sin and ask Jesus to forgive them."

~ CHAPTER SEVEN ~

Who's in Hell?

God never designed hell as a place for people; it was always His plan to have His children reside with Him. But when Adam and Eve disobeyed God's command not to eat the fruit from the tree of good and evil, He had to separate them from the tree of life so they would not live eternally in sin. God expelled them from the Garden of Eden which also separated them from the God who had created them. Jesus Christ, the Son of God, redeemed man from the bondage of sin, the grip of sickness, the power of Satan and eternal life in hell when He died on the cross to take our punishment for our sin. All who repent of their sin and receive Jesus Christ's forgiveness for their sins has their name recorded in the Lamb's Book of Life. Whoever does not have their name written in the Book of Life will spend eternity in hell. It is a very simple but profound truth. According to the Word of God, hell has been enlarged to accommodate the sinners who have refused to repent of their sin and acknowledge that Jesus is Lord. In Isaiah there are sins, or woes, that arouse the anger of God and bring His judgment, and hell has been expanded because of these transgressors.

"Woe to those who join house to house;
They add field to field,
Till there is no place
Where they may dwell alone in the midst of the land!
Woe to those who rise early in the morning,
That they may follow intoxicating drink;
Who continue until night, till wine inflames them!
Therefore Sheol has enlarged itself
And opened its mouth beyond measure;
Their glory and their multitude and their pomp,
And he who is jubilant, shall descend into it.
Woe to those who draw iniquity with cords of vanity,
And sin as if with a cart rope;
Woe to those who call evil good, and good evil;
Who put darkness for light, and light for darkness;
Woe to those who are wise in their own eyes,
And prudent in their own sight!
Woe to men mighty at drinking wine,
Woe to men valiant for mixing intoxicating drink,
Who justify the wicked for a bribe,
And take away justice from the righteous man!
Because they have rejected the law of the LORD of
hosts,
And despised the word of the Holy One of Israel.
Therefore the anger of the LORD is aroused against
His people"
(Isaiah 32:8, 11, 14, 18, 20-25).

Accumulating riches of the world without

compassionate giving is a sin. There is nothing wrong with having riches if you tithe according to the Word of God and give according to the Lord's leading. There are many rich people in this world that give to charitable causes, but their giving is meaningless because they do not acknowledge Jesus as Lord and Savior. Their works will be burnt up when they stand before God because all good works must have their foundation in Jesus Christ. "For no other foundation can anyone lay than that which is laid, which is Jesus Christ. Now if anyone builds on this foundation with gold, silver, precious stones, wood, hay, straw, each one's work will become clear; for the Day will declare it because it will be revealed by fire; and the fire will test each one's work, of what sort it is. If anyone's work which he has built on it endures, he will receive a reward" (1 Corinthians 3:11-14).

Getting drunk on wine and intoxicating drinks is a sin that will ensure you a place in hell because it leads to many other sins. Some men entice women to get drunk because alcohol impairs judgment. The woman becomes sexually promiscuous in a drunken state, and this serves the man's sexual agenda. Domestic and public violence is more prevalent in the drunken state, and drunk driving has needlessly snuffed out many lives. The Word of God is very explicit that drunkenness leads to depravity and ultimately to a life in hell. "Therefore do not be unwise, but understand what the will of the Lord is. And do not be drunk with wine, in which is dissipation; but be filled with the Spirit, speaking to one another in psalms and hymns and spiritual songs, singing and making melody in your heart to the Lord, giving thanks always for all things to God the Father in the name of our Lord Jesus Christ" (Ephesians 5:17-20).

Unbelief is another sin that Isaiah specifically targets as a pathway to hell. There are skeptical people that will only believe God exists if He gives them an outward sign. Jesus rebuked the scribes and Pharisees for demanding such signs. "Then some of the scribes and Pharisees answered, saying, 'Teacher, we want to see a sign from You.' But He answered and said to them, 'An evil and adulterous generation seeks after a sign, and no sign will be given to it except the sign of the prophet Jonah. For as Jonah was three days and three nights in the belly of the great fish, so will the Son of Man be three days and three nights in the heart of the earth'" (Matthew 12:38-40).

There are also people that chase after outward signs and wonders instead of chasing after God. They run from one ministry to another seeking the supernatural, and some are being deceived. Not all signs and wonders are from God, because the enemy can produce the same miracles. The false prophet will deceive a multitude of people. "He performs great signs, so that he even makes fire come down from heaven on the earth in the sight of men. And he deceives those who dwell on the earth by those signs which he was granted to do in the sight of the beast, telling those who dwell on the earth to make an image to the beast who was wounded by the sword and lived" (Revelation 13:13-14). Signs and wonders that are truly from God will accompany the preaching of the Gospel. "And He said to them, 'Go into all the world and preach the gospel to every creature. He who believes and is baptized will be saved; but he who does not believe will be condemned. And these signs will follow those who believe: In My name they will cast out demons; they will speak with new tongues; they will take up serpents; and if they drink anything deadly, it will by no means hurt them; they will lay hands on the sick, and they will recover'" (Mark 16:15-18).

Calling evil good and good evil, as well as putting darkness for light is a sign that hell is your eternal destination. The hearts of people are becoming colder and colder, and there is a greater gulf between God's children and Satan's children. This darkness is becoming like a thick fog when hearts become more hardened towards God's truth. "But know this, that in the last days perilous times will come: For men will be lovers of themselves, lovers of money, boasters, proud, blasphemers, disobedient to parents, unthankful, unholy, unloving, unforgiving, slanderers, without self-control, brutal, despisers of good, traitors, headstrong, haughty, lovers of pleasure rather than lovers of God, having a form of godliness but denying its power. And from such people turn away!" (2 Timothy 3:1-5).

People have become less compassionate and less loving because they have been desensitized towards the brutal violence, the heinous crimes, the rampant sexual sin, and the cruel injustices of the world. Most people do not consider God's hand of discipline as a judgment for disobedience to His commands. Instead they call it fate, bad luck, or even Mother Nature. The weather patterns speak loud and clear that God is trying to get mankind's attention. God controls the weather, and as sin abounds in a nation, the weather patterns are becoming more violent, causing more devastation and death.

The dramatic increase in tornadoes, hurricanes, and floods cannot be overlooked in our nation. These are the signs of the last days, yet most people are oblivious to this connection. Another sign that we are approaching the last days is the uprising in the nations that have deposed dictators. Egypt is an example where a world leader was overthrown in these uncertain times, and the Lord revealed this message to me before the toppling of Mubarak: *"The beginning of the alignment of the ten nations that will partner with the Anti-Christ has commenced. Nations that have previously aligned with Israel will no longer support her. Egypt is one. This uprising will see a change in leadership that will break the alliance with Israel. Egypt will come under Islamic rule, and she will no longer protect the borders into Israel. Arms and weapons will flow freely into Gaza. Forces of evil are at work in this nation."*

The world scene is like a drama unfolding on stage, and the curtain is about to open for the final scene. The Anti-Christ will negotiate a major peace treaty with Israel, and the world will be applauding this man for accomplishing such a great feat, and people will be lulled into this false sense of security that all is well in the world.

Operating in the wisdom of the world instead of the wisdom of God will bring about destruction and hell. The fear of God is the beginning of all wisdom, and God's wisdom is the solution to any situation that arises. The wisdom of the world seeks to please men and not to offend any religious, cultural or political group. The wisdom of the world says to permit same-sex couples to marry because we need to be tolerant of every one's choices and beliefs. The world says it is a crime to speak against homosexuality, but God says the sin is punishable by death in hell.

The wisdom of the world is forcing Israel to give up God's land so the Palestinians can have a separate state. God gave this land to the Israelites, and He is very jealous for His land! God's hand of judgment will come against every nation that tries to divide His land. The wisdom of the world takes bribes that remove the justice of the righteous, but God's wisdom is an advocate for the widow, the orphans, the oppressed and the downtrodden. The justice system in the United States has seen a steady decline, because of legal loopholes and lawyers who know how to manipulate the law. Our legal system has become corrupt because it has rejected and despised the law of the Lord. This is a path that will ensure a place in hell, but embracing God's Word will ensure salvation.

There are fallen angels chained in hell because they did not keep their proper domain in the realm for which God created them. Angels travel back and forth from heaven to earth, and they can take on human form. This is evidenced in scripture when the angels visited with Abraham and ate a meal with him. When certain angels saw how beautiful the women of the earth were, they procreated with them. Their offspring became a mixture of human and angel, which produced giants or nephilim in the land.

> "Now it came to pass, when men began to multiply on the face of the earth, and daughters were born to them, that the sons of God saw the daughters of men, that they were beautiful; and they took wives for themselves of all whom they chose. And the LORD said, 'My Spirit shall not strive with man forever,

for he is indeed flesh; yet his days shall be one hundred and twenty years.' There were giants on the earth in those days, and also afterward, when the sons of God came into the daughters of men and they bore children to them. Those were the mighty men who were of old, men of renown. Then the LORD saw that the wickedness of man was great in the earth, and that every intent of the thoughts of his heart was only evil continually. And the LORD was sorry that He had made man on the earth, and He was grieved in His heart" (Genesis 6:1-6).

As a result of this procreation of the angels with humans, the human race was about to be altered permanently. This was a perfect plan for Satan to destroy the human race because he knew that God had pronounced there would be hostility between him and the Messiah who would be born from the seed of a woman. If the seed of the woman was permanently altered through the procreation with fallen angels, then Satan could not be defeated.

God decided to destroy all mankind with a flood except Noah, his wife, their three sons and their wives. Eight people in all were preserved to continue the procreation of the earth, and Satan's plans were foiled. The angels that procreated with the daughters of men were cast into hell and placed in everlasting chains. "And the angels who did not keep their proper domain, but left their own abode, He has reserved in everlasting chains under darkness for the judgment of the great day; as Sodom and Gomorrah, and the cities around them in a similar manner to these, having given themselves over to sexual immorality and gone after strange flesh, are set forth as an example, suffering the vengeance of eternal fire" (Jude 6-8).

The Book of Ezekiel clearly states that the nations that come against Israel will come under divine judgment by God and will be cast into hell. In Ezekiel, Chapter Thirty-Two, there is a list of nations that are consigned to the pit of hell because of the terror they have perpetrated against Israel: Egypt, Assyria, Elam, Meshech, Tubal, Edom, and Sidonia. The modern day countries associated with this list in Ezekiel are respectively: Egypt, Syria, Iraq, Iran, Turkey, Jordan, and Lebanon. Ancient Egypt is still modern day Egypt. Assyria is Syria and parts of Iraq. Ancient Elam was Persia, which is current day Iran. Meshech and Tubal were sons of Japheth, Noah's third son. They settled in the land of Asia Minor which is current day Turkey. Edom was the land settled by the descendants of Esau which is the country of Jordan. Ancient Sidonia was Sidon and still exists in Lebanon today. All of these nations geographically surround Israel, and they all have fought against Israel from ancient times until current times.

In Ezekiel Chapters Thirty-Eight and Thirty-Nine there is a final battle called the Battle of Gog and Magog. Gog will be the chief prince of Meshech and Tubal, which will come against the land of Israel after the thousand-year reign of Jesus Christ in Jerusalem. The lists of nations that will join in this battle are as follows. Asia Minor is Turkey, ancient Persia is Iran, Ethiopia or Cush is Sudan and ancient Libya is still modern Libya. Gomer and Togarmah was eastern Asia Minor, which is also Turkey. According to the Book of Revelation, these nations will come from the four corners of the earth, which indicate there are four nations that are located in four geographic locations. Turkey is to the north of Israel, Sudan is to the south of Israel, Libya is to the east of Israel, and Iran is to the west of Israel.

Turkey, along with Iran, Sudan and Libya will make war with Israel. In that day, there will be a great earthquake in Israel, and mountains will be thrown down, and every wall will fall. In the confusion, the armies from Turkey, Iran, Sudan, and Libya will begin to kill each other. God will send down upon the troops flooding rain, great hailstones, fire and brimstone. The people of Israel will collect all the weapons of warfare and burn them as fuel for the next seven years, and they will plunder the armies. It will take seven months to bury all the dead to cleanse the land. After this Battle of Gog and Magog, the Great White Throne Judgment will occur, and all of the nations that plotted against Israel will be cast into hell.

According to God's Word, there are many people already in hell and many more are bound for hell. I was swimming at a lake one summer, and on the beach I noticed a young man with a large tattoo across his shoulders. In large script letters was the word HELLBOUND. I approached him and told him I was fascinated by his tattoo, which made him eager to talk with me. I asked him three simple questions. Have you ever told a lie? Have you ever used God's name as a swear word? Have you ever looked at a woman with lust? He very proudly answered yes to all of my questions. I explained to him that he was indeed hell bound, just as his tattoo declared. He vehemently declared that he was angry with God. I explained to him that God's anger was justified against him because of his sin, but his anger towards God was unjustified. I shared with him the Gospel message and went on my way so he could ponder his eternal destination. I prayed that one day he would repent from his sins and have his tattoo altered to HEAVENBOUND!

~ CHAPTER EIGHT ~

Demons and Spirits

Demons and evil spirits exist in the spiritual realm, and although we do not generally see them, their workings are quite evident in the lives of people. Most of Jesus' earthly ministry was casting out unclean spirits and spirits of infirmity. We cannot ignore the reality of the spiritual world and its effects upon people, but we also cannot be so focused on them that we are sensing demons everywhere. I have found the latter is usually not the case, because a lot of people refuse to acknowledge that fallen angels are demons. It is to the detriment of the body of believers to ignore the workings of the enemy. If we bury our heads in the sand, the evil spirits will not go away and forget we exist. On the contrary, we become a bigger target because of ignorance. Jesus warned us to be shrewd of the workings of the enemy. "Behold, I send you out as sheep in the midst of wolves. Therefore be wise as serpents and harmless as doves" (Matthew 10:16). It behooves us to take heed to this warning and be aware how these demons and spirits operate.

The spirit of deception is a mastermind of humanity. Demonic spirits observe the lives of God's children, and they record weaknesses, desires, likes and dislikes. They report all this information to the spirit of deception who devises a plan based on this information to deceive the individual. It becomes very easy for the person to become deceived because the deception is based on personal information. The spirit of deception can easily imitate the voice of God and make it sound very convincing. When the individual thinks he is truly hearing the voice of God, the spirit of deception has a foothold to con the believer. The only measuring rod that will keep you from deception is the Word of God and the witness of the Spirit. If something does not line up with the Word of God, then it is not from God! Once the spirit of deception has a foothold, then a lying spirit is added to the deception to keep the person believing the lies perpetrated by the enemy. Other people can unwittingly become pawns of the spirit world, and they confirm the lie, which then completely convinces a person that he or she is truly acting according to God's plan. Scripture clearly paints the picture of how a lying spirit works in conjunction with the spirit of deception.

> Then Micaiah said, "Therefore hear the word of the LORD: I saw the LORD sitting on His throne, and all the host of heaven standing by, on His right hand and on His left. And the LORD said, 'Who will persuade Ahab to go up, that he may fall at Ramoth Gilead?' So one spoke in this manner, and another spoke in that manner. Then a spirit came forward and stood before the LORD, and said, 'I will persuade him.' The LORD said to him, 'In what way?' So he said, 'I

will go out and be a lying spirit in the mouth of all his prophets.' And the LORD said, 'You shall persuade him, and also prevail. Go out and do so.' Therefore look! The LORD has put a lying spirit in the mouth of all these prophets of yours, and the LORD has declared disaster against you" (1 Kings 22:19-23).

All the prophets in the land, except Micaiah, prophesied that Ahab and Jehoshaphat would win the battle against Syria. The lying spirit had convinced all the prophets of the land to speak a false word, and the spirit of deception was upon Ahab to believe the prophecy. The reason it was effortless for Ahab to believe this false word from the prophets was because he coveted the land of Ramoth Gilead, and Ahab was unrelenting in procuring the land he desired.

His intense desire opened him up to believe the false prophecy; therefore, he was deceived. In the battle, Ahab was struck by a random arrow between the joints of his armor, and he died. These lying spirits were messengers sent to deceive Ahab, and their function has not changed over the ages. They unduly influence people by placing thoughts of sin in the minds of people. The mind is Satan's greatest battlefield, and he tries to control your thoughts by placing subliminal messages in your mind through television, music, magazines and other media.

Demons can directly place thoughts in your mind through your subconscious. Random thoughts of suicide, drugs, alcohol, sex or violence could be placed in your thoughts by a demon. It is important that when these thoughts come, that you discard them and recognize them as a tactic of Satan's cohorts. "For though we walk in the flesh, we do not war according to the flesh. For the weapons of our warfare *are* not carnal but mighty in God for pulling down strongholds, casting down arguments and every high thing that exalts itself against the knowledge of God, bringing every thought into captivity to the obedience of Christ, and being ready to punish all disobedience when your obedience is fulfilled" (2 Corinthians 10:3-6). "I beseech you therefore, brethren, by the mercies of God, that you present your bodies a living sacrifice, holy, acceptable to God, *which is* your reasonable service. And do not be conformed to this world, but be transformed by the renewing of your mind, that you may prove what *is* that good and acceptable and perfect will of God" (Romans 12:1-2).

The spirit of deception has caused people to veer from the truth of the Bible so that they begin to believe in heresy. A great heresy plaguing the religious world is that there is neither a heaven nor a hell. Another false doctrine that has spread is that there are many ways to heaven. Hell is a real place, and heaven is a real place, but there is only one way to get to heaven. "Jesus said to him, 'I am the way, the truth, and the life. No one comes to the Father except through Me'" (John 14:6). Any other teaching that says there are others ways to heaven are false and comes from a deceiving spirit. "Now the Spirit expressly says that in latter times some will depart from the faith, giving heed to deceiving spirits and doctrines of demons, speaking lies in hypocrisy, having their own conscience seared with a hot iron" (1Timothy 4:1-2).

The spirit of deception can also take people on a path in life that God never intended. This path may not necessarily be a sinful path; but it is not God's will for your life. Marriage is an excellent example because it was ordained by God, and it is good. But how many people pray and seek God's choice for a life-mate? The spirit of deception gathers all the information about you and then can place a man or woman in your path that matches all your desires and preferences for a mate. You think, without ever conferring with God, that he or she is God's choice for you based on your personal evaluation of the person. The spirit of deception is chuckling with glee because you took the bait along with the hook, line and sinker! The love relationship develops, and you proceed with the engagement and eventually marry; only to realize years down the road that you made a mistake. The deception could have been avoided if you asked God to make it clear if this man or woman was His choice for you.

Evil spirits gather information about you by listening to your words. They hear the words you speak and know your heart regarding a matter. "For out of the abundance of the heart the mouth speaks" (Matthew 12:34). It is important that you only speak good things. If you speak condemning words against another person or about yourself, the enemy will use your words to devise a plan for your detriment. Words are powerful, and what you speak releases power for life and death. "Death and life are in the power of the tongue, And those who love it will eat its fruit" (Proverbs 18:21). If you love to speak evil, then you will eat its fruit because you have given the enemy ammunition to use against you. "Even so the tongue is a little member and boasts great things. See how great a forest a little fire kindles! And the tongue is a fire, a world of iniquity. The tongue is so set among our members that it defiles the whole body, and sets on fire the course of nature; and it is set on fire by hell" (James 3:5-6). The tongue is set on fire by hell when the evil spirits use your own words to set Satan's plans in motion.

When you speak, you either release God to work in your life or you release Satan to work in your life. Jesus spoke of the importance of our words and gave us a warning: "A good man out of the good treasure of his heart brings forth good things, and an evil man out of the evil treasure brings forth evil things. But I say to you that for every idle word men may speak, they will give account of it in the day of judgment. For by your words you will be justified, and by your words you will be condemned" (Matthew 12:35-37).

Demonic spirits are observers of humanity. Their main focus is to keep a person blinded from the truth that Jesus Christ is Savior. Their methods include keeping people believing in false gods or believing there is no God at all. They also keep people so busy with work, hobbies, vacations and the latest luxury toys that they have no time for God. Evil spirits also keep people in poverty so that their main focus in life is obtaining food and clothing. The spirit of addiction as another ploy of the enemy to keep people addicted to drugs, alcohol and sex. Demonic spirits also create fear and doubt to paralyze the born again believer. So how do we prevent these evil spirits from gathering information about us and using it against us? Stay close to God by renewing your mind with the Word of God, pray for God's protection, worship God, ask God to search your heart to see if you harbor any wicked ways, and guard the words you speak.

There are multitudes of demonic spirits that have

particular assignments meant to destroy and cause havoc in people's lives. One of those spirits is a sexual spirit, and its main goal is to keep a person in sexual bondage through rape, incest, child molestation and pornography. This spirit can be a generational spirit that is passed down from one generation to the next as the result of the sin of a father or grandfather.

I know of a woman who viewed pornography as a small child when she accidently walked into the room where her mother was watching it. A few days after viewing the pornography, she began to see a demon perched on her bedroom window. She was a small child, and her mother did not believe her when she told her about the demon. Soon after being exposed to the pornography and the appearance of the demon, a family member began sexually abusing her at age six. The sexual abuse continued all through her childhood by various men because she was defenseless as a child.

As an adult, she has looked back upon her life and said she always felt like she was a target for these sexual predators. She was a target because the demon was released into her life as the result of the pornography. She also had a predisposition for the sexual abuse because, as a child, her mother was also sexually abused by her father.

This sexual demon was passed from one generation to the next and continued the cycle of incest in her family. Unfortunately, this sexual demon was passed onto her daughter who was also sexually abused at age five. Three generations of little girls were sexually abused because a demon was released into their lives by a male member of the family who chose to force an incestuous relationship with his daughter. Scripture says that the results of the sins of a father can reach three or four generations, and that is exactly what has happened. "The LORD is longsuffering and abundant in mercy, forgiving iniquity and transgression; but He by no means clears the guilty, visiting the iniquity of the fathers on the children to the third and fourth generation" (Numbers 14:18). If there is a history of sexual abuse within a family, the power of the Name of Jesus and His shed blood can break this generational curse so it does not continue. Tell the sexual spirit to leave in the Name of Jesus and break the generational curse by invoking the name of Jesus.

There are also spirits of addiction whose main purpose is to keep a person craving drugs and alcohol to the point that they lose control of their ability to turn away from the substance. Bars and parties with drugs and alcohol are where these demons hang out waiting to prey on their next victim. Substances that altar the mind and the emotions are open doors for the spirit of addiction to enter, and demonic spirits gain entrance through drugs. Marijuana users are known to have experienced multiple personalities, which are the outward signs of the presence of demons.

Heroin and crack cocaine users report the sensation of worms crawling in their veins. This is also a demonic experience. The spirit of addiction associated with alcohol is a little less subtle. It is, nonetheless, just as deadly. This spirit works progressively, unlike the spirits that are associated with drugs. Little by little, this spirit of addiction takes more control of the person as they drink, until one day they cannot go a day without a drink. There are many alcoholics that cannot control their drinking because the spirit of addiction has entered them. A bar is no place for a born again Christian.

A godly woman told me her story about being in a nightclub right after she got saved. Her husband was not saved yet. He still was going to nightclubs, and she felt it was her place to be by his side. The first time she went to the nightclub after she had been saved, three demons began to swirl around her, and she was paralyzed with fear. These demons knew she was a child of God, and they did not want her in their territory. After ten minutes of abject terror, she left the bar and never returned to those places again. These demons are real, and they do inhabit places like bars, nightclubs, crack houses and brothels.

The spirit of suicide is a demonic spirit whose purpose is to snuff the life out of their victim by convincing them to take their own life. This spirit works side-by-side with the spirit of depression and the demonic spirits associated with drugs and alcohol. The spirit of suicide becomes so strong within an individual that they feel their only recourse is to end their life. Desperation, hopelessness and sorrow are the emotions that are heightened by this spirit to incapacitate the person's mind, ultimately driving them to desperate measures. The pervading thought that is placed in the mind of the individual by the suicidal demon is that death is the only solution to the problem. When these strong thoughts become overwhelming, call upon the name of Jesus, and the spirit must leave. There is power for deliverance from suicide, alcohol and drugs in the Name of Jesus, because He came to set the captives free from the power of the enemy. Use His name! Cry out, Jesus!

Unclean spirits torment those who do not belong to God. "Also a multitude gathered from the surrounding cities to Jerusalem, bringing sick people and those who were tormented by unclean spirits, and they were all healed" (Acts 5:16). Tormenting spirits can drive a person to self-injury such as cutting or body mutilation. They cause anxiety, depression, fear, and a feeling of hopelessness. These unclean spirits can cause fits of uncontrollable rage that can lead to violence and even murder. There are serial killers who seem to lead normal lives until they have a strong desire to kill because a demonic spirit takes control. Unclean spirits can cause convulsions, epileptic seizures and sicknesses in an individual. These are also cast out in the name of Jesus just by calling out His name

There are demons and evil spirits assigned to churches. The purpose of these demons is to destroy a church through either creating a church split, a lack in finances, or causing a pastor to fall into sin. They create strife, disunity, gossip and division among the brethren. These spirits draw people that are argumentative, divisive and controlling into a congregation to try to destroy a church that is effective for the kingdom of God. These people stir up trouble in one church, do as much harm as they can and then move to the next church. These church jumpers never stay in one church for very long because they refuse to submit to the authority of the pastor or the elders. Most spirit-filled pastors are very aware of the forces of evil that come against his flock and staff. Prayer and worship are the keys to keeping these spirits at bay so God's work is accomplished. "Hear my cry, O God; Attend to my prayer. For You have been a shelter for me, A strong tower from the enemy. So I will sing praise to Your name forever" (Psalm 61:1, 3, 8).

~ CHAPTER NINE ~

Schemes of Satan

The Lord gave me two separate visions of Satan and Lucifer. First I will describe the vision the Lord gave me of Satan, which I included in my first book called *I AM the GOD that REVEALS*. Satan was black with what looked like large, semi-transparent black wings on his back. There were visible black veins running through his wings, similar to a bat's wings, but much larger. He was hunched over, and his face was vile and ugly.

Satan had black, scraggily long hair with sporadic pieces randomly sticking out of his head. His teeth were sharp and uneven. They protruded out of his mouth in jagged rows like shark's teeth, and he made biting movements with his mouth to frighten people. His skin was dark, greenish black with a slimy appearance like a sea serpent, and he had sharp claw-like hands.

In the vision of Lucifer, I saw a side-view of him, and he was very tall. He had golden wings on his back that glistened. Then Lucifer turned so that I could view him from the front, and I saw that his beauty was stunning. When I saw the front view of Lucifer, I began to cry because I remembered what

Satan looked like, and there was such a stark contrast. Lucifer had a smaller set of golden wings covering the front of him, and his feet appeared to be like shiny brass. His hair was a magnificent flow of golden waves that framed his tender face and his love for God was tangible as his eyes radiated the glory of God.

Then I saw Lucifer bowing before God on the throne, and Lucifer's worship was pure. Then he opened his mouth, and the most beautiful melodious sound came out. It was the sound of a multitude of musical instruments as he sang, twirled, and danced on the fiery stones before the throne. While Lucifer was worshipping, God rose from His throne to receive his praises and looked with delight at Lucifer. Although I did not see God the Father in this vision, I knew by the Spirit of God that He rose from His throne to receive Lucifer's worship. After this vision the Lord Jesus said: *"My child, this is how Lucifer looked before he decided to rebel against Me because of his pride. Lucifer became enamored with himself because of his beauty, his musical abilities, and his close proximity to My throne. He began to believe that he was better and more powerful than Me. People need to be warned not to become so enamored with their outward appearance, their abilities or intelligence. Also, be careful about spiritual pride because of a close relationship to Me."*

In the Bible, there are many names assigned to Satan that describe his character and function. God's people have disregarded the workings of Satan, and it has been to their detriment. The church has ignored Satan and his schemes; then they wonder why most of their sheep have been wounded so severely that they are ineffective for the kingdom of God.

If you have a deadly enemy, then you should be aware of his plans and take appropriate action not to get wounded or killed. If you know Jesus Christ as your Savior, then you have a deadly enemy, and he is at war with you on a regular basis. If Satan can incapacitate you and make you ineffective for the kingdom of God, then he has won. Satan can make you unproductive through sickness, family issues, financial woes, and sin. If Satan can keep you so preoccupied with these worries, then your constant focus is on how to resolve these issues and not on winning souls for Christ. Studying the names of Satan in scripture will give you an advantage to know his tactics so you can counter-attack and be on the offensive instead of the defensive. The best strategy of war is to out maneuver your enemy and place them on the defensive! All great wars have been won using this strategy. If you are successful in keeping your enemy on the defense, then you will win the war. The church has not been taught this strategy; however, it is biblical to know your enemy and have a plan of attack. God said through the prophet Hosea, "My people are destroyed for a lack of knowledge" (Hosea 3:6). By studying the names of Satan, we gain knowledge of our greatest enemy, and we can formulate a counter-attack.

Lucifer

How you are fallen from heaven,
O Lucifer, son of the morning! (Isaiah 14:12)
Son of man, take up a lamentation for the king of
Tyre, and say to him,
Thus says the Lord GOD:
"You were the seal of perfection,

Full of wisdom and perfect in beauty.
You were in Eden, the garden of God;
Every precious stone was your covering:
The sardius, topaz, and diamond,
Beryl, onyx, and jasper,
Sapphire, turquoise, and emerald with gold.
The workmanship of your timbrels and pipes
Was prepared for you on the day you were created.
"You were the anointed cherub who covers;
 I established you;
You were on the holy mountain of God;
You walked back and forth in the midst of fiery
stones.
You were perfect in your ways from the day you were
created,
Till iniquity was found in you.
"By the abundance of your trading
You became filled with violence within,
And you sinned;
Therefore I cast you as a profane thing
Out of the mountain of God;
And I destroyed you, O covering cherub,
From the midst of the fiery stones.
"Your heart was lifted up because of your beauty;
You corrupted your wisdom for the sake of your
splendor;
I cast you to the ground" (Ezekiel 28:12- 17).

Lucifer was a cherubim created by God who was
perfect in beauty and full of wisdom. He resided in the Garden

of Eden, and he walked on the fiery stones on the mountain of God. His garment was adorned with every precious gemstone, and he played musical instruments to worship God. Lucifer was perfect in all of his ways until he became prideful about his beauty. His wisdom became corrupt when he became elevated in his own eyes and desired to ascend to heaven to be like God. Lucifer wanted his position exalted above where God had established him on the holy mountain in the Garden of Eden. God inhabited this holy mountain much like He did with Moses, and God created Lucifer to worship Him on this mountain. Lucifer was not satisfied with his position and desired his throne to be in heaven. As a result of insolence and pride, Lucifer was cast out of the mountain of God to the earth below. Before his insurrection against God, Lucifer was also able to convince one third of the angels to rebel. As a result, Lucifer became Satan, and the fallen angels became demons.

One of the trademarks of Satan is to arouse pride in a person, especially in the body of Christ. One of his most prevalent strategies is to make a person feel spiritually superior to others because of the gifts of the Holy Spirit. The Holy Spirit imparts spiritual gifts for power to be His witnesses, but Satan entices a person to feel superior to their brothers and sisters in Christ. Soon there is division among the saints, and a spirit of disunity prevails.

Once pride enters, it opens the door for other spirits to come in, namely a deceiving spirit. Once a deceiving spirit has a foothold, you are a pawn in Satan's plans. This deceiving spirit can whisper anything in your ear and make it sound like it came from God. You will be doing and saying things you insist are from God, but they are not! I met with a woman who insisted that God gave her a ministry to go into various churches to correct the pastors. I knew immediately that this action was not from the Spirit of God, but rather a deceiving spirit rooted in pride. A person full of pride will refuse to submit to spiritual authority and will run from one church to another with this deceiving spirit. It will take a person with the gift of discernment to uncover the deceiving spirit and cast it out. Knowing that pride is a tactic of Satan, use this check list, and ask God to reveal your true heart regarding pride.

1. Do you feel spiritually superior to others because of your gifts?
2. Do you have a difficult time receiving correction?
3. Do you find it difficult to submit to authority?
4. How many churches have you attended in the last five years?
5. Do you find it necessary to correct others and point out their faults?
6. Must you always win at something?
7. How well do you get along with your brothers and sisters in Christ?

The Holy Spirit will uncover any pride in your life so you can repent. If you choose not to repent or to ignore the warnings of the Holy Spirit, then I can guarantee that God will humble you with His hand of discipline. The choice is yours. Lucifer was cast to earth because of his pride, and his ultimate demise will be in the lake of fire for all eternity. If God did not spare His created cherub who was perfect in all his ways, He will not spare you if there is pride! He who has an ear, let him hear what the Spirit is saying to the church.

Serpent

"Now the serpent was more cunning than any beast of the field which the LORD God had made. And he said to the woman, 'Has God indeed said, You shall not eat of every tree of the garden?' And the woman said to the serpent, 'We may eat the fruit of the trees of the garden; but of the fruit of the tree which is in the midst of the garden, God has said, *You shall not eat it, nor shall you touch it, lest you die.'* Then the serpent said to the woman, 'You will not surely die. For God knows that in the day you eat of it your eyes will be opened and you will be like God, knowing good and evil'" (Genesis 3:1-4).

Satan either transformed himself into a serpent, or he inhabited the body of the serpent to tempt Eve to partake of the forbidden fruit. One of Satan's functions is to tempt a person to sin by whatever means that will appeal to that person. First he placed doubt in Eve's mind about what God said. He uses the same tactics today by making people doubt whether the entire Bible is true. Satan reasons with people that parts of the Bible may be true, but other parts just don't apply to the believer today because they are not culturally relevant. I have heard people say that we don't live under the Old Covenant, so we do not have to follow the Ten Commandments. This is the same old trick that Satan used when he whispered into Eve's ear, "Did God really say that?"

As believers, we live under the New Covenant, but

Jesus did not come to abolish the law; He came to fulfill the law. We follow the Ten Commandments because Jesus said, "If you love Me you will keep My commandments" (John 14:15).

Satan can take the word of God and alter it by a few words so that it still sounds like the word of God, but it is not. That is why it is important to know scriptures. Only by knowing scriptures can you discern if the pure word of God is being preached.

Satan also appealed to Eve's desire to obtain knowledge that she was not meant to have. His ways have not changed; he just chooses another generation to deceive. Satan tantalizingly says to the married man, "Having an affair will be exciting. The wife is not as sexy since she gained those extra pounds, and a little fling on the side won't hurt anyone if you keep it a secret." He whispers in the ears of the teenager, "It is okay to have that first beer, nothing will happen." Or he says, "You will be popular if you smoke marijuana, and having sex with your boyfriend won't hurt anyone as long as you use protection." These are all things that God never intended you to partake of, but the enemy uses your flesh to make you desire them. Eve had lust in her eyes when she viewed the fruit, and the desire became so overwhelming that she ate it. She chose to believe the lies of Satan and succumb to the lust of her flesh, and the result was catastrophic. Guard yourself from the lies of Satan so your sweet communion with God is not broken.

Devil and Tempter

"Then Jesus was led up by the Spirit into the wilderness to be tempted by the devil. And when He had fasted forty days and forty nights, afterward He was hungry. Now when the tempter came to Him, he said, 'If You are the Son of God, command that these stones become bread.' But He answered and said, *'It is written, Man shall not live by bread alone, but by every word that proceeds from the mouth of God.'* Then the devil took Him up into the holy city, set Him on the pinnacle of the temple, and said to Him, 'If You are the Son of God, throw Yourself down. For it is written: *He shall give His angels charge over you, and, In their hands they shall bear you up, Lest you dash your foot against a stone.'* Jesus said to him, 'It is written again, *You shall not tempt the LORD your God.'* Again, the devil took Him up on an exceedingly high mountain, and showed Him all the kingdoms of the world and their glory. And he said to Him, 'All these things I will give You if You will fall down and worship me.' Then Jesus said to him, 'Away with you, Satan! For it is written, *You shall worship the LORD your God, and Him only you shall serve.'* Then the devil left Him, and behold, angels came and ministered to Him" (Matthew 4:1-11).

Satan tempted Jesus to show His true identity with signs and wonders before it was time for Him to be revealed as the Christ. It was set in the annals of time the exact day when Jesus' identity would be revealed, and before the world was formed, the day was set when Jesus would be crucified for the sins of mankind. Satan tried to thwart those plans by tempting Jesus to reveal His identity before the Father's perfect time. This temptation came at the very beginning of Jesus' ministry, before the Apostles were chosen and trained by Jesus. If Jesus would have succumbed to Satan's temptation and revealed Himself as the Son of God, then the church would not have been born to take the Gospel message to the ends of the earth throughout the ages!

God's timing is always perfect, but the devil will try to foil God's timing by whispering things in your ear. Satan will try to get you to jump ahead or lag behind God's plans. If you desire to know God's plans and His timing to fulfill them, then you must do what Jesus did. He spent time fasting and praying so He could hear from His Father in heaven. One of the most powerful tools to overcome the schemes of the devil is to pray and fast, but this takes discipline. If you truly want to be a powerful vessel of the Lord, then your flesh must be submitted to your spirit so you can rise above your carnal desires. Jesus had been fasting for forty days when the devil tempted Him to turn the stones into bread. The bread would have satisfied Jesus' fleshly hunger, but at the same time would have identified Him as the Son of God. Jesus' Spirit had to rise above His bodily hunger so He would not succumb to this temptation.

Satan's principal method in his evil endeavors is to tempt people beyond their ability to choose the right thing. When Satan attacks people with temptation, it is important to use God's Word as a way to overcome the temptation. "No temptation has overtaken you except such as is common to man; but God is faithful, who will not allow you to be tempted beyond what you are able, but with the temptation will also make the way of escape, that you may be able to bear it" (1 Corinthians 10:13). The key to this scripture is taking the way of escape that God provides to overcome the temptation. Sin is a choice. First, it is conceived in the mind, and then it is dwelt upon until action is finally taken. When the thought first enters the mind, then it must be discarded and not dwelled upon. This is one way of escape. If the sin is a spontaneous knee jerk reaction like anger, swearing or lying, then there must be a renewing of the mind in that area.

You renew your mind with the Word of God. "But now you yourselves are to put off all these: anger, wrath, malice, blasphemy, filthy language out of your mouth. Do not lie to one another, since you have put off the old man with his deeds" (Colossians 3:8-9). God's Word is power, and people are blinded to the authority they possess through the spoken Word of God. Quoting scriptures out loud releases God's power as a way of escape from the temptation and the sin. Satan does not want you to use the Word of God because he knows his tactics will not work on you! Jesus defeated Satan's temptation by using the scriptures to release the power of God, and we should follow Jesus' example. Verbalizing scriptures releases God's power to defeat the schemes of Satan!

The morning I was writing this section, I had emotional turmoil in my heart, and there was an oppressive demonic heaviness that was tangible. I prayed and asked the Lord to remove the emotional chaos and oppression and fill me with His joy and peace. The Lord spoke three simple words to me: *"Psalm Twenty-Three."* I recited the Psalm and felt some of the oppression lifting. The Holy Spirit prompted me to recite it a second time, and the oppression completely left. The third time I recited it, the Lord filled with His peace and joy. The words of the Psalm had sunk deep within my spirit to set me free, but I needed to press into God's freedom with a determined persistence. So often we only pray once and think that the matter is in God's hands when it truly rests in our perseverance in prayer to see the matter resolved. I know the Lord allowed me to experience this so I could be a testimony to the power of God's Word and to the necessity of pressing into God for His deliverance from the enemy. Satan's schemes are destroyed by the spoken Word of God, and we must use this weapon of warfare just as Jesus did!

Satan

"And the Lord said, 'Simon, Simon! Indeed, Satan has asked for you, that he may sift you as wheat. But I have prayed for you, that your faith should not fail; and when you have returned to Me, strengthen your brethren'" (Luke 22:31-32).

Satan wanted to put Peter through a sieve to prove to God that when pressure was applied to Peter, he would fail the test of loyalty to Jesus. In ancient times, after the wheat was harvested, it was taken to the threshing floor to separate the wheat from the stalk. The threshing floor was a large stone elevated on a hill, and the wheat was beaten with a threshing instrument to remove it from the stalk. Then the wheat was thrown up in the air, and the chaff, which was lighter, would be blown away by the wind. The final step in the threshing process was to put the wheat through a sieve to remove any dirt that got mixed in with it while on the threshing floor. Satan wanted to prove to God that there was still dirt in Peter's life, and he wanted to sift him.

Satan still does the same thing today. He can cause situations to arise in our lives that expose the dirt and filth in our hearts. Satan delights in revealing our sin and then rubbing it in our faces. He makes you feel guilty and unworthy to be called God's child. But Jesus reminds us through this scripture that He was praying for Peter's faith to be strong and for him to return to the Lord after he failed the test. Satan will sift us to expose our dirt, but Jesus is always interceding for us so we will repent and turn back to Him.

Although Satan wants to sift us to uncover our filth, Jesus is the One who truly sifts us to purify us. The place where the wheat is separated from dirt and the chaff is our hearts. This is where God's takes up His holy residence because we are the temple of the Lord.

Beelzebub

"Now when the Pharisees heard it they said, 'This fellow does not cast out demons except by Beelzebub, the ruler of the demons.' But Jesus knew their thoughts, and said to them: 'Every kingdom divided against itself is brought to desolation, and every city or house divided against itself will not stand. If Satan casts out Satan, he is divided against himself. How then will his kingdom stand? And if I cast out demons by Beelzebub, by whom do your sons cast them out? Therefore they shall be your judges. But if I cast out demons by the Spirit of God, surely the kingdom of God has come upon you. Or how can one enter a strong man's house and plunder his goods, unless he first binds the strong man? And then he will plunder his house. He who is not with Me is against Me, and he who does not gather with Me scatters abroad'" (Matthew 12:24-30).

Beelzebub or Baal-Zebub was the name of a god of the Philistine city of Ekron. When King Ahaziah was injured, he sent a messenger to inquire of Baal-Zebub whether he would recover. God sent Elijah to deliver His message of judgment upon the king for inquiring of a false god instead of inquiring of the God of Israel. The Lord pronounced a death sentence upon King Ahaziah and said he would not come down from his bed and he would surely die. It is a very serious thing to enquire of other gods or spirits, and the penalty is death.

Satan worship, witchcraft, sorcery, ancestor worship, wizards, spiritists, and mediums will all be judged by God with a death sentence. Those who practice New Age with sweat lodges, vision quests, healing energy exchanges, talking circles, and group meditations are like King Ahaziah because they refuse to call upon God for answers. God will judge them for their unbelief and cast them into a lake of fire. Beelzebub will deceive people to the end and will convince them that their practices and rituals are spiritual, but God has the final say.

Those who contact familiar spirits by calling upon the dead through mediums are dabbling in the occult, and their father is Beelzebub or Satan. Ghost chasing is another popular activity among the youth, and they think it is harmless and fun. On the contrary! I was called to come and minister to a Christian family because their two year old was hearing voices telling him to jump out of his bedroom window. I knew they were experiencing the presence of demons in their home, but I did not know how they gained entrance. Upon interviewing the other family members, the connection became obvious. The teenage son had been ghost chasing at a popular graveyard and said he experienced a demonic presence. The time frame when the demon manifested itself to the teenager was the same time the two year old heard the voice of a demon telling him to jump out the window. The teen repented of his sin, and I laid hands and prayed over the entire family, and they were set free from the demonic presence in their home.

Roaring Lion and Adversary

> "Be sober, be vigilant; because your adversary the devil walks about like a roaring lion, seeking whom he may devour" (1 Peter 5:8).

There is good reason why Satan is referred to as a lion and an adversary. In nature, lions tend to hunt mostly by night or in the early mornings so they are not visible to their prey. Satan operates in the darkness so his deeds are hidden, but God has delivered us from the darkness. "He has delivered us from the power of darkness and conveyed *us* into the kingdom of the Son of His love, in whom we have redemption through His blood, the forgiveness of sins" (Colossians 1:13-14).

Lions hunt animals that are some of the fastest on the planet. An antelope can achieve a top speed of around sixty miles-per-hour and maintain it effortlessly, but there are two things that help the lion when hunting these swift antelope. First, they are incredibly good at hiding and phenomenally patient. Second, while the antelopes are physically fast, they are not as mentally sharp as the lions, and they do not learn from their mistakes. Satan is good at hiding and incredibly patient, and he relies on people disregarding past sins and mistakes. He is exceptionally sly in disguising his tactics to entice a person into the same sin. Like the lion, he crouches down and patiently waits to go in for the kill. Throughout the Bible, the sins of people were recorded so we can learn from their mistakes and not repeat them. Will we give the roaring lion the upper hand by ignoring destructive behaviors, or make a conscious decision not to walk in the same sin? It is a matter of life and death.

Ruler of Darkness

"For we do not wrestle against flesh and blood, but against principalities, against powers, against the rulers of the darkness of this age, against spiritual hosts of wickedness in the heavenly places" (Ephesians 6:12).

Satan is identified as a ruler of darkness, prince of the power of the air, the god of this age, and the ruler of this world. Although we live in this world, and Satan has power in this realm, his power does not exceed God's power. As children of God, we have God's power over the enemy. It is our responsibility to be aware of the devil's schemes in the earthly realm and wield God's power by invoking the name of Jesus. We need to draw close to the Lord and develop an intimate relationship with Him.

To the degree and magnitude that you know God, be to the degree He holds you accountable for the way you live your life. To ignore God's revelation of Himself expressed through His creation and through the Bible will not hold you without excuse when you stand before a holy God. The more intimately you know God, the more He holds you accountable for your actions and even your thoughts. Thoughts play a vital role in the manner in which we live out our lives.

When our lives do not conform to God's plans, He disciplines His sons and daughters to produce holiness and righteousness. "My son, do not despise the chastening of the LORD, Nor be discouraged when you are rebuked by Him. Now no chastening seems to be joyful for the present, but painful; nevertheless, afterward it yields the peaceable fruit of righteousness to those who have been trained by it" (Hebrews 12:5, 11).

I can say from personal experience that God does discipline His children for having evil thoughts about people. I was battling with reoccurring thoughts that were ungodly, and I knew originated from the ruler of darkness. At times I would call upon the name of Jesus, and the thoughts would dissipate, but at other times I would entertain the evil thoughts. It was a constant battle of the mind, and I knew these were harmful thoughts from the enemy. One night these thoughts were strongly invading my mind and I decided to permit them and not call upon the name of Jesus. It was a willful act on my part to entertain these thoughts because I knew the power of Jesus to set me free from the works of the enemy, yet I did not call upon Jesus. Within an hour, a storm rolled in and the electricity to my home was cut off. I thought it was a widespread power outage until the next morning revealed another scenario. A tree had fallen on the power line close to my house and took out my electricity. I knew immediately that God was disciplining me for dwelling on the evil thoughts. The Lord knows the power of the enemy over the mind, and if those thoughts remain unchecked, they could become a regular part of my subconscious, and I could eventually act on them. The Lord was revealing to me that to entertain ungodly thoughts cuts off His power in my life, just as the power was cut off in my home.

There are many polluted thoughts people battle with on a regular basis such as suicide, revenge, past rejection, feeling inadequate, illicit sex, past abuse, racial injustices and social inequalities. Dwelling on these thoughts are perilous because they produce a gamut of emotions such as anger, sorrow, self-pity, lust, and hatred. Once these emotions are established and get a foothold, there is a temptation to act on these emotions.

Temptation begins in the mind, moves to the emotions and then proceeds to the body. Sin is first conceived in the mind and then worked out in the flesh, once a thought has been entertained and accepted by the individual. The key to overcoming the temptation and sin is not to allow the evil thought to take up residence by reflecting on it and accepting it. God has given us the way of escape regarding evil thoughts and temptation so they are cut off at the root. The answer is the name of Jesus. There is power and authority in Jesus' name, and when His name is spoken, the enemy will flee.

By consciously redirecting your thoughts towards

Jesus, the wicked thoughts will quickly leave because darkness and light cannot reside in the same place. God desires to fine-tune the thoughts of His children so we can have the mind of Christ. The process of being conformed to the image of Christ in body, soul, and spirit is called sanctification. The mind is a vital part of the sanctification process whereby we are made holy and are set apart unto God. When impure thoughts pervade the mind, call upon the name of Jesus and you will be set free from temptation and sin.

Although Satan is called the ruler of this world, the universe belongs to God! You can have a divine connection to the God of the universe through Jesus. You can have the inside scoop, the inside story, and the inside knowledge because of your connection to Jesus. Nothing goes on in this world that God doesn't know about, and you can have access to that information through Jesus and the Holy Spirit. All that is required is an intimate relationship with God the Father and Jesus Christ. God's children need to know about this divine connection and how much God desires to reveal things for your protection against the god of this age.

Thief, Father of Lies, Murderer

"The thief does not come except to steal, and to kill, and to destroy. I have come that they may have life, and that they may have it more abundantly" (John 10:10).

"You are of your father the devil, and the desires of your father you want to do. He was a murderer from the beginning, and does not stand in the truth, because there is no truth in him. When he speaks a lie, he speaks from his own resources, for he is a liar and the father of it" (John 8:44).

Satan is a thief whose purpose is to rob people of their salvation so that when they die, they will go to hell. He professes many lies to deceive people. One such lie is that there is no heaven or hell, no demons, and Satan does not exist. He lulls people into ambivalence about the existence of a spiritual world and cons people into believing there is no life after the death of the body. Satan whispers these lies, "When you die, you die. There is no life after death. So eat, drink and be merry! Do what is right in your own eyes and only seek to please yourself." When he gets people to buy into these lies, then he has signed their death warrant to hell for all eternity. Satan is a murderer, a thief, and a liar.

Wicked One and Enemy

"Then Jesus sent the multitude away and went into the house. And His disciples came to Him, saying, 'Explain to us the parable of the tares of the field.' He answered and said to them: 'He who sows the good seed is the Son of Man. The field is the world, the good seeds are the sons of the kingdom, but the tares are the sons of the wicked one. The enemy who sowed them is the devil, the harvest is the end of the age, and the reapers are the angels'" (Matthew 13:36-39).

Satan is wicked because he is constantly conniving and coming up with ways to hurt God's people. He is the enemy, and he never ceases from his wickedness. Satan strategically places his children among God's children to cause havoc. When good seeds and bad seeds are planted together, the bad plants cannot be pulled out without disrupting the roots of the good plant. People question why bad people seem to get away with evil while good people suffer. "Righteous *are* You, O LORD, when I plead with You; Yet let me talk with You about *Your* judgments. Why does the way of the wicked prosper? *Why* are those happy who deal so treacherously?" (Jeremiah 12:1). The answer is that Satan has sown his wickedness in the world, and God will not separate the wicked from the good until the end of the age.

Son of Perdition

"Let no one deceive you by any means; for that Day will not come unless the falling away comes first, and the man of sin is revealed, the son of perdition, who opposes and exalts himself above all that is called God or that is worshiped, so that he sits as God in the temple of God, showing himself that he is God" (2 Thessalonians 2:3-4).

"While I was with them in the world, I kept them in Your name. Those whom You gave Me I have kept; and none of them is lost except the son of perdition, that the Scripture might be fulfilled" (John 17:12).

Scripture mentions two people who are called the son of perdition; Judas Iscariot who betrayed Jesus, and the Antichrist who will declare he is God. Perdition means "ruin or loss; someone who is physically, spiritually and eternally damned." Judas Iscariot was eternally damned to hell because of the decision he made to betray Jesus. The Antichrist will also be eternally damned when he battles Christ at the Battle of Armageddon. Any person or nation that battles against Jesus and Israel will be eternally damned just like Judas and the Antichrist. God wants people to know that if they strive against His Son Jesus Christ, they will be punished.

Angel of Light

"For such *are* false apostles, deceitful workers, transforming themselves into apostles of Christ. And no wonder! For Satan himself transforms himself into an angel of light. Therefore *it is* no great thing if his ministers also transform themselves into ministers of righteousness, whose end will be according to their works" (2 Corinthians 11:13-15).

There is a group of false ministers that have been deceived by Satan who has appeared as an angel of light. Embracing homosexuality, abortion, and the ecumenical movement that believes all religions can reach a common ground are just some of the ways Satan has transformed ministers into false apostles. In order for these ministers to accept these false doctrines, Satan comes to them as an angel of light and uses tolerance, political rights, and freedom of religion as his tool. These ministers are deceived because they truly believe they are showing the love of God by embracing the sins of homosexuality and abortion. You can love someone straight into hell by withholding God's truth. True love says that I care enough about you to speak the truth, even if it hurts for a season. In the end, however, the truth will produce righteousness.

Belial

"Do not be unequally yoked together with unbelievers. For what fellowship has righteousness with lawlessness? And what communion has light with darkness? And what accord has Christ with Belial? Or what part has a believer with an unbeliever?" (2 Corinthians 6:14-15).

Belial is an epithet for Satan that means "worthlessness, without profit, and wickedness," all of which describe the devil. The Apostle Paul used stark contrasts to show that believers should not be yoked together with unbelievers. Light and darkness, righteousness and lawlessness, and Christ and Satan are diametrically opposed in every way. The believer and the unbeliever are also completely opposite. One of Satan's schemes is to integrate his children with the children of God to persuade them to follow the ways of his world. This is an old tactic that he has used for centuries, and sadly, the ploy still works.

Evil One

"And do not lead us into temptation, But deliver us from the evil one. For Yours is the kingdom and the power and the glory forever. Amen" (Matthew 6:13).

One of the most horrendous strategies of the evil one

is to cause intense strife among people so that there is a spirit of unforgiveness in their hearts. Unforgiveness opens the door for spirits that can cause depression, anxiety, bitterness, and sickness. There was a young woman who was battling with depression, anxiety, and variety of sicknesses. She called me and wanted to talk because her mental and physical condition had worsened, and she was desperate. On the way to see her, I prayed and asked God what I should say to her. The Holy Spirit revealed to me that her problems were rooted in her unforgiveness she had for her father who had abandoned her. When I got to her home, she was weeping and was an emotional wreck. I explained to her that the entrance for the sickness and the deep depression was a result of her unforgiveness for her father. She prayed with me to forgive her dad and the depression, anxiety, and sickness immediately left her body. Later, the young woman wrote me a note and told me the Holy Spirit gave her this scripture immediately after I had left. "And whenever you stand praying, if you have anything against anyone, forgive him, that your Father in heaven may also forgive you your trespasses. But if you do not forgive, neither will your Father in heaven forgive your trespasses" (Mark 11: 25-26).

Dragon

"And another sign appeared in heaven: behold, a great, fiery red dragon having seven heads and ten horns, and seven diadems on his heads. His tail drew a third of the stars of heaven and threw them to the earth. And the dragon stood before the woman who was ready to give birth,

to devour her Child as soon as it was born"
(Revelation 12:3-4).

Dragon is another term used to describe Satan, and his activities are evident from this scripture. He convinced one third of the angels to rebel against God, and they were cast to the earth and became demons. Satan tried to have Jesus killed by stirring up Herod to kill all baby boys under the age of two. He placed paranoia and fear in the heart of Herod that another king would rise to power and take his position. This paranoia became so overwhelming in his life that Herod had his wife, sons, and other family members killed. From these two activities we can see the power and influence Satan had to convince angels to rebel against God and a king to murder his family. Never underestimate Satan's influence over the mind. The Bible gives us the solution to vile thoughts placed in our minds by Satan. "Finally, brethren, whatever things are true, whatever things *are* noble, whatever things *are* just, whatever things *are* pure, whatever things *are* lovely, whatever things *are* of good report, if *there is* any virtue and if *there is* anything praiseworthy—meditate on these things" (Philippians 4:8).

Accuser of the Brethren

"So the great dragon was cast out, that serpent of old, called the Devil and Satan, who deceives the whole world; he was cast to the earth, and his angels were cast out with him. Then I heard a loud voice saying in heaven, 'Now salvation, and strength, and the kingdom of our God, and the power of His Christ have come, for the accuser of our brethren, who accused them before our God day and night, has been cast down'" (Revelation 12: 9-10).

The devil goes before God and accuses people of the sin he knows they have committed because his demons give detailed reports of their sin. Imagine this scenario: Satan is standing before the throne and mockingly tells God that a woman named Samantha has lied about her salary on her income tax report. God retrieves His records on Samantha and affirms that she is one of His own. He looks at the date on the records that his angel had recorded and says to Satan, "Samantha belongs to me, and she has confessed this sin, and it is covered under the blood of My Son. Be gone with you, Satan, you have nothing on her!" It is important to confess our sins daily and ask Jesus to forgive us so the devil has no dirt on us and there is no hidden darkness within us. In the last days, the devil and his demons will not have access to heaven to accuse the brethren, and the devil and his demons will be confined to the earth and the sea. It will be a time of great distress for the inhabitants of the earth because Satan knows his time of power will be coming to an end.

Leviathan

"In that day the LORD with His severe sword,
great and strong,
Will punish Leviathan the fleeing serpent,
Leviathan that twisted serpent;
And He will slay the reptile that is in the sea"
(Isaiah 27:1).

Leviathan is a "serpent or other large sea monster and also a symbol of Babylon." The description of this twisted sea serpent in Job portrays the characteristics of Satan. He is strong and cannot be restrained by mortal man. He has the ability to speak in a way that is appealing in order to cover his vile nature. He will use the Antichrist to speak flattery to make a covenant with Israel through peace negotiations. Scriptures prophesy that the Antichrist will be killed with the sword, but the power of Satan will resurrect him. Even though the sword reaches him, it cannot prevail. The only sword that will prevail against Leviathan is the great and severe sword of the Lord. Satan is full of pride, and he is king over all people filled with pride. He has a very vile appearance, and his formidable appearance is meant to shock and frighten whoever views him. Intimidation is one of the tactics of Satan. Although we are no match for Satan, we have the power of Christ within us who has already defeated him. Knowing your power and authority in Christ is the key to defeating Satan's intimidation and power.

Satan is constantly planning and scheming to cause destruction and pain in the lives of God's children, but through Jesus Christ, we have the victory! Satan is full of hatred towards Jesus, and he will do atrocious things to get revenge. One of his tactics to exact his vengeance on mankind is to attack the sacred covenant of marriage that God established in the Garden of Eden. If Satan can destroy a marriage and a family, then he can slowly eradicate the representation that God established in His Word about Christ and the church.

The enemy took his vengeance upon me and my children by destroying our family, but through the crisis, I became spiritually strong. The suffering I experienced drew me intimately close to the Lord, but for many years, I hid my scars because there was a certain shame in not being able to save my marriage. Part of my final healing process was to expose my scars. My scars are evidence of my empathy. If you have scars, it is because you were once wounded, are now healed, and you can empathize with those experiencing the same trials.

Jesus has scars! The scars on His hands, feet, and side are evidence of His compassion for mankind. Jesus lovingly said this to me: *"My scars remain as a reminder that I paid the price for the sin of mankind. I displayed My scars to the disciples so they would know it was Me. When I return, people will look upon the One they have pierced, and they will mourn when they see My scars. Patricia, don't hide your scars. I don't hide Mine. You have made it through an intense wounding, and now it is time to share your story. Let your scars show so I can minister to women who have been wounded by unfaithful husbands, separation or divorce. Through your scars, I will pour out My healing anointing to set the captives free."*

After fifteen years of a great marriage and two beautiful children, I was completely blind-sided by what was to take place. When I stood at the altar and took my wedding vows, I stood before a holy God and promised that I would stand by this man no matter what life brought. Standing at the altar that moment and in the years to come, I never imagined my husband could ever betray me in the arms of another woman. Then the day came when the bomb was dropped, and the reality of his adultery was exposed. I will never forget the day.

When I received the news, I dropped to my knees and began to sob. I was numb, in shock, and deeply wounded by his immense betrayal. I called upon the Lord and said, "Now, what do you want me to do? He has committed adultery!" Immediately the Lord said, *"You must forgive him."* I quickly countered the Lord, "I don't have it in my heart to forgive him! But if You place the forgiveness in my heart, then I will." The Lord said without hesitation, *"It is done."* At that moment God divinely filled my heart with forgiveness for both my husband and the woman. Because I chose to forgive them, God spared me from the anguish of bitterness and hatred that overtake so many people who chose not to forgive.

For several more years my husband continued in the adulterous relationship while still living in our home, and the emotional pain was threatening to consume me. My heart was heavy with anguish at the constant rejection as he continued in the adulterous relationship. Each night he left, I had to make a choice. Either fall to my knees and bitterly cry or fall to my knees and worship the Lord. There were times I wept bitterly, and my emotions were in an upheaval. But when I chose to worship God, His beautiful peace enveloped me like a warm comforting blanket. I quickly learned the awesome power of worshipping God in all circumstances and discovered there was enormous triumph in worship.

It is easy to worship God when everything is rosy, but when your life is crumbling, worshipping God is needed the most because His power is manifested in your life. There is great victory in praising the Lord because the battle belongs to Him. I sang praises to the Lord, and His holy presence would fill my room and minister to me. During this painstaking ordeal, I grew so intimately close to my Lord Jesus and my Papa Father God. I would not trade the time I spent with the

Lord for anything in the world! God used my intense trial to strengthen my relationship with Him as I conversed with Him and worshipped Him. One day I was worshipping the Lord, and He spoke this to me: *"The enemy is going to try and kill you with cancer, but do not fear; I will deliver you."* Several months after receiving the message from the Lord, another bomb was dropped in my life. I was diagnosed with HPV, which is a sexually transmitted disease and the number-one cause of cervical cancer in women.

My doctor called me into his office and explained my diagnosis, and with great anguish I had to tell him about my husband's adultery. Along with his adultery, I was now infected with an incurable disease that he transmitted to me because of his infidelity. I felt like this was the knockout punch of the enemy, until I remembered what the Lord had spoken to me. God's peace filled me even when the HPV was progressing into precancerous and then cancerous cells because I had faith Jesus was going to heal me.

God instructed me to attend a healing service in Pittsburgh and two women from New York also attended at the Lord's instructions. Hours before the healing service began, these two women prayed for me without knowing I had cervical cancer. When they laid hands on me, I felt the spirit of cancer exit my body, and I knew Jesus had healed me. Within a week after the healing service, I had an appointment with my doctor to have another biopsy to determine how the cancer was advancing. I explained to my doctor that I was healed by Jesus Christ, and the new biopsy would confirm it. Two weeks later, the results of the new biopsy were back from the lab, and my doctor said this with amazement, "Patricia, there are no signs of cancer, and you no longer have HPV!"

Jesus Christ delivered and healed me from the cancer and the HPV! Satan planned to kill me with cancer, but Jesus warned me about his schemes. The Lord instructed me where to go to receive my healing, and then He healed my body from two incurable diseases! I kept praying God would intervene and that our marriage would be restored, but my husband kept making decisions that were completely destroying the marriage. The constant emotional pain of rejection was a heavy weight that was threatening to consume me emotionally. The Lord clearly spoke to me that I could not minister to people through the grid of my emotional pain, and I needed to be set free.

God chose a very unique way to set me free. I was attending a service at a small Pentecostal church where the gifts of the Holy Spirit were freely flowing. A woman at the front of the church spoke a message in tongues. Immediately after she spoke it, the Holy Spirit said to me: *"Listen carefully to the interpretation, because this message is for you."* Within seconds, another woman gave this interpretation. "There is a person here today whose heart has been pierced by an arrow. Today I will remove that arrow, and you will be set free from the pain that has been gripping you." As soon as she spoke the message, I felt an enormous weight lift from my heart, and I was gloriously set free from the intense emotional pain of the years of adultery.

There may be someone who has intense emotional pain, and God wants to set you free. There are many hurting from adultery, separation or divorce. You may see yourself through my story, and there is healing in knowing that you are not the only one. Let your tears flow, for this is the beginning of your healing. Jesus wants to set you free from the pain and the bitterness, but first you must decide to forgive. Your freedom and deliverance depends on your forgiveness. Take the first step and ask the Lord to place His forgiveness in your heart for your offender. Then ask the Lord to set you free from the pain. Allow Him to restore your joy, peace and love; for nothing is impossible with God!

The Lord completely restored my joy, peace and love because I chose to forgive my first husband's adultery. Although I was convinced that I would serve the Lord as His single handmaiden, Papa Father had other plans for me. While attending a healing seminar, I met the man who Yahweh divinely chose for me. Will swept me off my feet by loving Yahweh with all his heart and loving me with Papa's agape love. We were married on Passover as a reminder of His great sacrifice and love for us. Together in unity, we minster as a husband and wife team, preaching the full gospel message of salvation, healing and deliverance.

~ CHAPTER TEN ~

Gate to Heaven

Gates are important in scripture. There is a gate to heaven, gates to hell and gates of the city. Jacob saw the gate to heaven where the angels were descending and ascending on a ladder in a constant flurry of activity.

> "Now Jacob went out from Beersheba and went toward Haran. So he came to a certain place and stayed there all night, because the sun had set. And he took one of the stones of that place and put it at his head, and he lay down in that place to sleep. Then he dreamed, and behold, a ladder was set up on the earth, and its top reached to heaven; and there the angels of God were ascending and descending on it. And behold, the LORD stood above it and said: 'I am the LORD God of Abraham your father and the God of Isaac; the land on which you lie I will give to you and your descendants. Also your descendants shall be as the dust of the earth; you shall spread abroad to the west and

the east, to the north and the south; and in you and in your seed all the families of the earth shall be blessed. Behold, I am with you and will keep you wherever you go, and will bring you back to this land; for I will not leave you until I have done what I have spoken to you.' Then Jacob awoke from his sleep and said, 'Surely the LORD is in this place, and I did not know it.' And he was afraid and said, 'How awesome is this place! This is none other than the house of God, and this is the gate of heaven!'" (Genesis 28:10-17).

Scripture speaks of an angel going before the Israelites to bring them safely into the Promised Land where this gate to heaven was located. "Behold, I send an Angel before you to keep you in the way and to bring you into the place which I have prepared" (Exodus 23:20). Before the Israelites entered the Promised Land, God instructed Joshua to circumcise all the men of Israel. "Then the LORD said to Joshua, "This day I have rolled away the reproach of Egypt from you. Therefore the name of the place is called Gilgal to this day" (Joshua 5:9).

The reproach of Egypt removed from them was their worship of false deities. In Egypt, the primary deity was Osiris who was the god of the dead and the lord of the underworld. The Apis bull was worshipped as the incarnation of Osiris. This black bull had a white diamond on its forehead, the shape of an eagle on its back, and the shape of a scarab beetle under its tongue. This live bull was worshipped by the Egyptians as Osiris, and while the Israelites sojourned in Egypt for four-hundred years, they also learned to worship this deity.

The circumcision of the Israelite males at Gilgal identified them as worshippers of the God of Abraham, Isaac, and Jacob and removed the reproach of their idol worship. After they were circumcised, they kept the Passover on the fourteenth day on the plains of Jericho as a remembrance that God had delivered them from the bondage of Egypt and the death angel. On the same day, the manna from heaven ceased, and they ate the produce of the land. God was preparing them to enter the land that He promised to Abraham, Isaac, and Jacob.

Right after the Passover, Joshua had an encounter with the Commander of the army of the LORD. This Commander was a theophany or an appearance of Jesus Christ before He came to this earth as the Son of man. "Then the Commander of the LORD's army said to Joshua, 'Take your sandal off your foot, for the place where you stand is holy.' And Joshua did so" (Joshua 5:15). What made this land so holy and sacred that Jesus commanded Joshua to remove his sandals? They were about to enter the one place on the face of the earth where the gate to heaven had been identified by Jacob hundreds of years earlier. Jericho was the entrance into the Promised Land, and the next cities that were conquered were Ai and Bethel. Jacob saw the gate to heaven at Bethel which literally means the House of God. God was about to give the land that was identified as the gate to heaven to His chosen people Israel. The Redeemer of all humanity would open up the gate to heaven that all may have an opportunity to enter in. There is only one gate to heaven, and Jesus is the door!

"Then Jesus said to them again, 'Most assuredly,

I say to you, I am the door of the sheep. All who ever came before Me are thieves and robbers, but the sheep did not hear them. I am the door. If anyone enters by Me, he will be saved, and will go in and out and find pasture. The thief does not come except to steal, and to kill, and to destroy. I have come that they may have life, and that they may have it more abundantly'" (John 10:7-10).

Hundreds of years later, Jeroboam, the King of Israel, would set up a golden calf in Bethel so the people would not go to Jerusalem to worship God. At this point in history the kingdom had been divided into ten tribes following Jeroboam and two tribes following Solomon's son Rehoboam. Jeroboam did not want the people traveling to Jerusalem to celebrate the Passover because he feared they would commit their allegiance to the house of David and Rehoboam.

Jeroboam reestablished the same idol worship of Egypt that the people had been delivered from at Gilgal when God rolled away the reproach of Egypt. They began to sacrifice animals to the golden calf, and Jeroboam told the people that this golden calf was the god that brought them out of Egypt. God declared that this act was more evil than all who ever came before Jeroboam. "Go, tell Jeroboam, Thus says the LORD God of Israel: 'Because I exalted you from among the people, and made you ruler over My people Israel, and tore the kingdom away from the house of David, and gave it to you; and yet you have not been as My servant David, who kept My commandments and who followed Me with all his heart, to do only what was right in My eyes; but you have done more evil than all who were before you, for you have gone and made for yourself other gods and molded images to provoke Me to anger, and have cast Me behind your back'" (1 Kings 14:7-10).

It is very significant that Jeroboam chose Bethel to set up a golden calf because it was the physical place that was identified with the gate to heaven. There was a spiritual battle that occurred when the land was possessed by pagan worship. It was not by chance that Jeroboam chose Bethel as a location to reinstate the idolatry of Egypt. He was influenced by high demonic powers to erect the altar and the golden calf. When Jeroboam set up this pagan worship, there was a war in the heavens between the angelic and the demonic forces. Every time the people sacrificed to the golden calf at Bethel, they empowered the demonic forces to continue the battle in the heavens against God's angels. Idol worship of any kind empowers demonic spirits, just as worshipping God empowers the angels.

God really opened up my eyes to the modern meaning of having other gods or idol worship during a prayer meeting. This is such a golden nugget of truth that He wants people to understand so it empowers them. Jesus taught these principles to His disciples, and the Holy Spirit opened up to me the fullness of His teaching.

> "No one can serve two masters; for either he will hate the one and love the other, or else he will be loyal to the one and despise the other. You cannot serve God and mammon. Therefore I say to you, do not worry about

your life, what you will eat or what you will drink; nor about your body, what you will put on. Is not life more than food and the body more than clothing? Look at the birds of the air, for they neither sow nor reap nor gather into barns; yet your heavenly Father feeds them. Are you not of more value than they? Which of you by worrying can add one cubit to his stature? So why do you worry about clothing? Consider the lilies of the field, how they grow: they neither toil nor spin; and yet I say to you that even Solomon in all his glory was not arrayed like one of these. Now if God so clothes the grass of the field, which today is, and tomorrow is thrown into the oven, *will He* not much more *clothe* you, O you of little faith? Therefore do not worry, saying, 'What shall we eat?' or 'What shall we drink?' or 'What shall we wear?' For after all these things the Gentiles seek. For your heavenly Father knows that you need all these things. But seek first the kingdom of God and His righteousness, and all these things shall be added to you. Therefore do not worry about tomorrow, for tomorrow will worry about its own things. Sufficient for the day *is* its own trouble" (Matthew 6:24-34).

When you see the word "therefore" in Scripture, you always want to go back to the previous verse to see what truth Jesus was about to unveil. Once Jesus made the statement that

God cannot be your master if your money is your master He said, "Therefore do not worry about food, drink, or clothing."

The biblical truth Jesus wanted to convey was that the things you worry about, you will eventually make into a god. If you worry about money, then money becomes your driving force and your god. If you worry about your health, then your well-being becomes your main concern and your god. If you worry about your children's welfare instead of trusting God, then your children become your god. If you worry about a job, then your career becomes a number one priority and your god. The things you worry about can become your god because you do not trust the God of the universe to work out all things for His glory. Worries are based on fear. You worry about money because you fear you will not have enough for food, clothes, and shelter. You worry about your health because you fear getting sick. You worry about your children because you fear something bad will happen to them. You worry about your job because you fear you may lose it.

Worries will eventually become a god in your life, and this biblical truth is threaded throughout the entire Bible. "Now when the people saw that Moses delayed coming down from the mountain, the people gathered together to Aaron, and said to him, 'Come, make us gods that shall go before us; for as for this Moses, the man who brought us up out of the land of Egypt, we do not know what has become of him'" (Exodus 32:1). The people were worried that Moses was not coming down from the mountain and they would not have a leader. The Israelites were so conditioned to a slave mentality and having a master that they became apprehensive about not having a leader. They convinced Aaron to make a gold calf that would be their god. Worshipping the calf was a familiar way of life for them because they had worshipped the many gods of the Egyptians.

Just as God commanded the Israelites to forsake their familiar ways, God is calling us to forsake our old familiar ways of worrying and put our confidence and hope in Him. He is calling us to a new thing which requires a greater walk of faith and a deeper trust in Him. Stop worrying, stop fearing the unknown, and stop panicking about uncharted territories. We need to resist being like the Israelites who did not trust the God of the universe. They did not trust God who had delivered them from the bondage of Egypt, parted the Red Sea, provided manna and quail to eat, and supplied water from the rock. How easy it is to forget God's provision and protection of yesterday, last week, or last year. When we forget God's goodness in our lives, we become just like the Israelites who resorted to fear and worry, which resulted in another god.

King Saul also permitted his fear and worry to become another god in his life.

> "Now Samuel had died, and all Israel had lamented for him and buried him in Ramah, in his own city. And Saul had put the mediums and the spiritists out of the land. Then the Philistines gathered together, and came and encamped at Shunem. So Saul gathered all Israel together, and they encamped at Gilboa. When Saul saw the army of the Philistines, he was afraid, and his heart trembled greatly. And when Saul inquired of the LORD, the

LORD did not answer him, either by dreams or by Urim or by the prophets. Then Saul said to his servants, 'Find me a woman who is a medium, that I may go to her and inquire of her.' And his servants said to him, 'In fact, *there is* a woman who is a medium at En Dor.'" (1 Samuel 28:3-7).

Saul was worried about the Philistine army, and his heart trembled greatly with an extraordinary amount of dread. Saul was accustomed to hearing from God through Samuel the prophet, but Samuel was dead. Saul had also previously heard God through dreams or by the urim and thumin. The urim and the thumin were two stones behind the breastplate of the high priest that were cast like dice and determined the will of God in a situation. Saul enquired about the Philistines. When he did not get an answer from God, he became frantic. God was testing Saul, but he let panic and worry drive him to seek the witch of Endor for an answer. Seeking mediums was strictly forbidden by God, but Saul chose this method because he was afraid that the Philistines would defeat Israel. How often do we allow fear to enter when we do not get an answer from God right away? Will we press into God through prayer and wait on God's response, or will we let our anxiety create another solution that is worldly and not God's answer?

Before the Apostle Paul was converted on the Damascus road, he permitted worry to create another god that led him to hunt and kill the Christians. "Then Saul, still breathing threats and murder against the disciples of the Lord, went to the high priest and asked letters from him to the synagogues of Damascus, so that if he found any who were of the Way, whether men or women, he might bring them bound to Jerusalem" (Acts 9:1-2).

Saul was a Pharisee that was proud of his position of authority and power, but Jesus condemned the religious leaders for this. When Jesus was teaching and ministering, the Pharisees hated Him because they were concerned that the multitudes would follow Him and they would lose their position and influence. Saul was not focused on the true God of Israel; he was focused on his own power, authority, and position that enabled him to hunt and kill the Christians.

When you focus on position and power rather than focusing on Jesus, you have made another god that is rooted in pride. There are signs in a church leader that indicate whether he is worshipping the god of power. A church leader that belittles people under his or her authority, or that is threatened by someone's knowledge of God's Word indicates he is focused on power. He can become jealous of those who have spiritual gifts, and he purposely becomes detached from these spirit-filled people who manifest God's power. These church leaders are worshipping another god. Beware of them! A true servant of the Lord is humble, peaceable, and rejoices when the flock is growing in the Word and in the Spirit.

There is no room for false gods in our lives. Jesus taught us to seek the kingdom of God first and His righteousness, and everything else will be given to us by the Father in heaven. The Father's kingdom has a physical gate, and that gate to heaven is located in the heaven of heavens. This physical gate was revealed to Jacob in Genesis and to John in Revelation. The Lord said to me: *"When a child of God dies, they are escorted through the gate of heaven by one of My angels. My servant Jacob saw this angelic activity when I showed him the gate to heaven in a dream."*

Scriptures confirm that angels do indeed escort godly people to their heavenly destination. "So it was that the beggar died, and was carried by the angels to Abraham's bosom" (Luke 16:22). There is only one physical gate to heaven, and there is only one spiritual gate to heaven. Jesus is the spiritual gate, and He is the only way to have eternal life in heaven. "Jesus said to him, 'I am the way, the truth, and the life. No one comes to the Father except through Me.'" (John 14:6).

~ CHAPTER ELEVEN ~

Location of Heaven

There is a specific place in the universe where heaven is located, and the bible clearly indicates that it is an upward direction. "For He looked down from the height of His sanctuary; From heaven the LORD viewed the earth" (Psalm 102:19). There are three layers of the heavens. The first heaven is the earth's atmosphere; the second heaven contains the other galaxies, and the third heaven is where God resides on His throne. The Apostle Paul was taken up to the third heaven where he witnessed marvelous things but was not permitted to divulge the wondrous vision. "I know a man in Christ who fourteen years ago—whether in the body I do not know, or whether out of the body I do not know, God knows—such a one was caught up to the third heaven. And I know such a man—whether in the body or out of the body I do not know, God knows—how he was caught up into Paradise and heard inexpressible words, which it is not lawful for a man to utter" (1 Corinthians 12:2-4).

Most people desire heaven as their final destination, and God has established a place called Paradise for all those who believe and receive Jesus as their Lord and Savior. The

Bible explains how and when God established this place called Paradise, but most often we refer to this place as heaven. The story begins in the Book of Luke when Jesus tells the narrative of a rich man and Lazarus.

> "There was a certain rich man who was clothed in purple and fine linen and fared sumptuously every day. But there was a certain beggar named Lazarus, full of sores, who was laid at his gate, desiring to be fed with the crumbs which fell from the rich man's table. Moreover the dogs came and licked his sores. So it was that the beggar died, and was carried by the angels to Abraham's bosom. The rich man also died and was buried. And being in torments in Hades, he lifted up his eyes and saw Abraham afar off, and Lazarus in his bosom. Then he cried and said, 'Father Abraham, have mercy on me, and send Lazarus that he may dip the tip of his finger in water and cool my tongue; for I am tormented in this flame.' But Abraham said, 'Son, remember that in your lifetime you received your good things, and likewise Lazarus evil things; but now he is comforted and you are tormented. And besides all this, between us and you there is a great gulf fixed, so that those who want to pass from here to you cannot, nor can those from there pass to us.'" (Luke 16:19-26).

Notice in this scripture that Lazarus was carried, and

the rich man was buried. One was carried up, and the other was buried below. Lazarus was carried by angels to a sweet place of rest, and the rich man was buried and went to horrible place of torment. Hades is defined as "the world of the dead as if a subterranean retreat including its accessories and inmates, grave, hell, pit." The Lord clearly spoke these words to me to correct what has been erroneously taught about the location of Hades and Abraham's Bosom: ***"Abraham's Bosom has never been beneath the surface of the earth. The great fixed gulf between Hades and Abraham's Bosom was the heavens. Notice that the rich man looked up and saw Abraham and Lazarus afar off. Abraham's Bosom was a place in the heavens that I established for all the righteous to go. The place was called Abraham's Bosom because he is the father of all those who would have faith in God. Scripture also states that Elijah went up to heaven in a whirlwind; he did not go down into the bowels of the earth.*** "Then it happened, as they continued on and talked, that suddenly a chariot of fire appeared with horses of fire, and separated the two of them; and Elijah went up by a whirlwind into heaven" (2 Kings 2:11).

The place that Elijah went was Abraham's Bosom, where all the other Old Testament saints were waiting until the Messiah made a way for them to enter Paradise. When Jesus was transfigured on the mount, Moses and Elijah appeared to Jesus, and they discussed these final details about Paradise, the place God had established before the beginning of time. As long as the Israelites were offering the blood of goats and bulls for sin, the doors to Paradise were closed. Jesus, the perfect, sinless Lamb of God would sacrifice His life and shed His blood to take away the sin of the world. Sin had separated man from

God in the Garden of Eden, but Jesus' shed blood would restore man with God in Paradise. Paradise in Greek is *paradeisos* which means "a park; specifically an Eden, a place of future happiness." Jesus said to the thief on the cross, "Assuredly, I say to you, today you will be with Me in Paradise" (Luke 23:43). The tree of life is in Paradise. "He who has an ear, let him hear what the Spirit says to the churches. To him who overcomes I will give to eat from the tree of life, which is in the midst of the Paradise of God" (Revelation 2:7).

Paradise could not be established until the finished work of the cross was complete, and Jesus' blood was in the heavenly tabernacle. Jesus told His disciples that He was going to prepare a place for them. "Do not let your heart be troubled. Believe in Elohim and believe in me. There are many rooms in my Father's House, and if not I would have told you so. For I go to prepare a place for you. And if I go and prepare a place for you, I will come again for you and take you with me, that where I am, you may be also" (John 14:1-3 AENT). The place that Jesus was preparing was Paradise which is located in the third heaven. Only the blood of the perfect Lamb of God could atone for the sin of mankind by completely removing it, and the Book of Hebrews explains how this was accomplished.

> "But Christ came as High Priest of the good things to come, with the greater and more perfect tabernacle not made with hands, that is, not of this creation. Not with the blood of goats and calves, but with His own blood He entered the Most Holy Place once for all, having obtained eternal redemption. For if

the blood of bulls and goats and the ashes of a heifer, sprinkling the unclean, sanctifies for the purifying of the flesh, how much more shall the blood of Christ, who through the eternal Spirit offered Himself without spot to God, cleanse your conscience from dead works to serve the living God" (Hebrews 9:11-14).

When did Jesus ascend to Paradise and sprinkle His blood in the heavenly sanctuary? At what point was Paradise open for all those who had died before the cross and were waiting in Abraham's bosom? The answer is found in scripture on the resurrection day of Christ. "Jesus said to her, 'Do not cling to Me, for I have not yet ascended to My Father; but go to My brethren and say to them, I am ascending to My Father and your Father, and to My God and your God'" (John 20:17). Jesus told Mary not to cling to Him because He had not yet ascended to His Father. But, eight days later, Jesus told Thomas to touch His hands and His side to dispel his doubt about Jesus resurrection. "And after eight days His disciples were again inside, and Thomas with them. Jesus came, the doors being shut, and stood in the midst, and said, 'Peace to you!' Then He said to Thomas, 'Reach your finger here, and look at My hands; and reach your hand here, and put it into My side. Do not be unbelieving, but believing'" (John 20:26-27).

Sometime between the morning of the resurrection, when He instructed Mary not to touch Him and the eighth day when He permitted Thomas to touch Him, Jesus ascended to heaven and sprinkled His blood in the heavenly sanctuary for the remission of all sin. This ascension is not to be confused with

Jesus final ascension on the Mount of Olives forty days after His resurrection. This first ascension was to atone for the sins of mankind by presenting His blood in the heavenly sanctuary because without the shedding of blood, there is no remission for sin. Scripture seems to further indicate that the doors to Paradise were not open on the first day of Jesus resurrection because the bodies of dead saints were witnessed walking in the streets of Jerusalem. "And the graves were opened; and many bodies of the saints who had fallen asleep were raised; and coming out of the graves after His resurrection, they went into the holy city and appeared to many" (Matthew 27:52-53).

Before Jesus ascended into Paradise with His blood, he also descended into the lower parts of the earth which would explain the delay of His first ascension to present His blood in the heavenly sanctuary.

> "But to each one of us grace was given
> according to the measure of Christ's gift.
> Therefore He says:
> *'When He ascended on high,*
> *He led captivity captive,*
> *And gave gifts to men.'*
> (Now this, *"He ascended"*— what does it mean
> but that He also first descended into the
> lower parts of the earth? He who descended
> is also the One who ascended far above all
> the heavens, that He might fill all things.)"
> (Ephesians 4:7-10).

Jesus was on a mission to fulfill everything that had been prophesied and written about Him. He descended into

Hades to retrieve the keys of Hades and Death from Satan, which gave people victory over the bondage of sin and death. "Do not be afraid; I am the First and the Last. I am He who lives, and was dead, and behold, I am alive forevermore. Amen. And I have the keys of Hades and of Death" (Revelation 1:17-19). Once Jesus had retrieved the keys of Hades and Death, He ascended to Paradise with His life-giving blood and securely placed it in the heavenly sanctuary. Jesus then led all those who were in Abraham's Bosom into Paradise. This was a moment in history that all the prophets and patriarchs had waited for with great anticipation. They waited in Abraham's Bosom until the day their Messiah Jesus Christ redeemed them with His blood and escorted them to this splendid place called Paradise.

This Paradise or heaven is the dwelling place of God and all who have eternal life through Jesus Christ until the New Jerusalem comes down from heaven. After the Great White Throne Judgment, there will be a cataclysmic event, and God will destroy the first heaven and the first earth. He will then begin again with everything new. God originally intended on living with man until Adam and Eve's sin separated them from God. When God creates the new heaven and the new earth, it will be restored to the likeness of original Garden of Eden where God dwelt with Adam and Eve.

All things will have come to a completed circle when the New Jerusalem comes down from heaven. It began with God and will be completed with God. This was His cosmic plan that no one could circumvent, not even Satan and his demons. God's plan to dwell with humanity was established in the beginning and no delays, setbacks, sin or rebellion will thwart

His divine blueprint for humanity. "Then I, John, saw the holy city, New Jerusalem, coming down out of heaven from God, prepared as a bride adorned for her husband. And I heard a loud voice from heaven saying, 'Behold, the tabernacle of God is with men, and He will dwell with them, and they shall be His people. God Himself will be with them and be their God'" (Revelation 21:2-3).

The Holy city of Jerusalem will descend down from the third heaven where it has been prepared by God and waiting for this set time in history. There will be no sun or moon to light up the New Jerusalem. With the new heaven and the new earth, there will be no constraints of time or space like there were in the old heaven and earth because there is no sun or moon to govern the days. Traveling to and from the far away galaxies will be a reality for God's children because we will be able to travel like the angels do. We will be able to go from one distant place to another very quickly because there are no constraints of time and space with our glorified bodies.

God's throne will be in the New Jerusalem, and there will be no temple because God the Father and Jesus Christ will reside there. There will be a beautiful river of life that flows from the throne of God, and on each side of the river, there will be a tree of life. This is the same tree of life that Adam and Eve were not permitted to partake of once they sinned. Each month, this tree will bear twelve different fruits for God's children to enjoy. The physical description of the New Jerusalem is stunning according to scriptures.

There will be twelve gates, each made from a single large pearl, and the names of each of the twelve tribes of Israel will be inscribed on each gate. There will be twelve layers of foundation that construct the walls surrounding the city. Each layer will be made of a different precious stone, and the names of the twelve apostles will be inscribed on each of the foundations. The streets will be made of pure gold that glisten and look like glass. The New Jerusalem will be the final dwelling place of God, and the new earth will be the final dwelling place of all who have received Jesus as Savior. The new earth will no longer have a sea, so it will be expanded to accommodate all of God's children. Everyone dwelling in the newness of God's plans will have their glorified body so the workings of this new earth will not resemble the old earth. This paradise will have all elements of the Garden of Eden, and God will dwell with mankind once again.

~ CHAPTER TWELVE ~

The Record Room

The Spirit of God revealed to me that there is a Record Room in heaven where there are a multitude of books stored. The Spirit of God said: "***Every person has a record, and your personal volume has information that is unique to you. Your worship is recorded in heaven. Your prayers are recorded in heaven. Your deeds are recorded in heaven. Your giving is recorded in heaven. This book contains your name, your birth date and time of birth. It contains the date you repented and received Jesus as Savior. Your volume has your complete genealogy that is traced to Adam.***" Our individual genealogies are recorded in heaven, so we can view our family tree and adopted children who never knew their biological parents will discover their true parentage. Children who were born out of wedlock and never knew their father will get a chance to discover who fathered them.

Jesus' genealogy is listed in the Gospel of Matthew and the Gospel of Luke, and I always pondered why it was so important that His descendants were recorded. Jesus was predestined to fulfill certain things that were prophesied about

Him in the Old Testament, and His genealogy proved that He was the awaited Messiah. Jesus' genealogy list in the Gospel of Matthew is through Joseph's lineage, and the one listed in the Gospel of Luke is through Mary's lineage. Both genealogies were important because one's Jewishness was passed through the mother, yet one's tribal inheritance was passed through the father. "Now Jesus Himself began His ministry at about thirty years of age, being (as was supposed) the son of Joseph, the son of Heli" (Luke 3:23).

The Jerusalem Talmud stated that Mary was the daughter of Heli, which clears up the misconception that the genealogy in Luke belonged to Joseph. Joseph was a son-in-law, and in those days would have been referred to as a son. Jesus' genealogy in the book of Luke was important because the Messiah was promised to descend physically from Abraham and from David. The Lord Jesus said this to me: *"My genealogy as recorded in the Word of God proves I am a descendant of David, a descendant of Abraham and Adam. This fulfills scriptures that were prophesied about Me. I was a Jew by birth through Mary, My mother and Joseph adopted Me as his son. An adopted son had all the legal rights of a son. My legal right to the throne of David came through Joseph's lineage even though he was not my biological father.*

Solomon was in Joseph's lineage and so was Jeconiah. My servant Jeremiah prophesied that no descendants of Jeconiah would ever sit on the throne of David. Since Joseph was not My blood father; then a descendant of Jeconiah never took David's throne." Speaking of Jeconiah, "Thus says the LORD: 'Write this man down as childless, A man who shall not prosper in his days; For none of his descendants shall prosper, Sitting on the throne of David, And ruling anymore in Judah'" (Jeremiah 22:30). *My legal right to the throne of David came through Joseph, but My Jewish birthright to the throne of David came through My mother Mary. This has been a stumbling block for many Jews, but My Word is Truth."*

What we learn about both of Jesus' genealogies is that God always keeps His Word! The angel prophesied that Mary's Son named Jesus would reign as King on the throne of David, and His kingdom would never end. "And behold, you will conceive in your womb and bring forth a Son, and shall call His name JESUS. He will be great, and will be called the Son of the Highest; and the Lord God will give Him the throne of His father David. And He will reign over the house of Jacob forever, and of His kingdom there will be no end" (Luke 1:31-33). We also learn that if it is written in the Word of God; then it will happen! The Word of God is powerful, and God's Word will not return to Him empty.

God has plans for His children, and those plans were foreordained and recorded in one of the books in the Record Room. Before we were born, God shaped our future according to His plans, and it is our job to seek God's destiny for us.

> "Your eyes saw my substance,
> being yet unformed.
> And in Your book they all were written,
> The days fashioned for me,
> When as yet there were none of them"
> (Psalm 139:16).

"For we are His workmanship, created in Christ Jesus for

good works, which God prepared beforehand that we should walk in them" (Ephesians 2:10).

The Lord explained to me about the good works He has planned for each of His children: "*These good works which are recorded in a book are My perfect plan for an individual. My plans can be altered by choices made by My children. I cannot and will not bend someone's will to accomplish My work. If I have a designated work for my children and they make a decision that puts a stop to My plan, then their course has been altered.*

The Israelites were a prime example of this principle. I never intended them to wander in the wilderness for forty years. They were a stubborn people and I could not reward their rebellion with entrance into the Promised Land. An entire generation had their God-ordained plans altered by their decision to rebel against Me by revolting against My servant Moses. I have plans for all of My children. Some of My children are more pliable and willing to bend to My will, while others are more stubborn, like the Israelites. The more stubborn the person, the more I have to revise My plans for their life because they refuse to submit. A lack of submission to God will result in less heavenly rewards because your rewards are based on your work." "And behold, I am coming quickly, and My reward is with Me, to give to everyone according to his work" (Revelation 22:12).

The written record of one's life will establish these rewards. They will also determine one's punishment if your name is not written in the Book of Life. In My book of Revelation, books are opened that reveal the individual record of each person. Every person has a personal volume, even if their name is not written in the Book of Life. Their deeds will be recorded, both good and evil. At the Great White Throne Judgment, the Book of Life will be also opened as written proof that a name has not been recorded, and they will receive their punishment according to the evil deeds they have done. There will be many who insist their name has been written in the Book of Life; but the absence of their name will determine their final destination.

I want all to know that your eternal destination of heaven or hell is determined by your choices made on earth. There is no repentance of sin after death, as some false teachers are reporting. There is only one way to have eternal life in heaven, and that is to receive the forgiveness of sins through Jesus, My Son. I sent My Son to redeem mankind from the power of darkness and set them free from the bondage of sin. Every good deed done by an individual who is not saved by the Lamb of God is done in vain. Good deeds are only sanctified and acceptable to God through the blood of the Lamb, because salvation is found in no other.

There will be those who think their good deeds such as giving to the poor, building orphanages in foreign lands, or volunteering at a homeless shelter will land them a place in heaven. On the contrary! Those good deeds will be burned up by My Holy Fire when My righteous anger proceeds forth to repay the wicked for refusing My Son. It is not too late to submit to the cleansing blood of My Son. Start now and leave the past behind. Believe in your heart that Jesus died on the cross for your sins and on the third day He rose from the dead. Repent and confess your sins and ask Jesus to forgive you. Sins that have been recorded in your book in heaven before you got saved will be blotted out forever by the blood of the Lamb. The pages in your book will become as white as snow."

The angels record the information in the books in heaven, and God has personal knowledge of everything contained in these books. The Holy Spirit revealed to me that these books in heaven are written in ancient Aramaic, and in a vision, I saw one of these volumes in the record room. The cover of the book was gold with a beautiful, intricately embossed design. There were gemstones embedded on the front cover. There was a large ruby in the center of the cover of the book with smaller diamonds surrounding it creating a pattern. There was an angel holding this volume, and I pondered if it were mine. A mighty angel guarded the entrance to the Record Room, and only those angels that were authorized to gather information and record the personal data were permitted to enter.

The Lord said: *"There are many secrets recorded in the volumes in heaven. When it is time for one of My secrets to be revealed from the record room, I send an angel to impart the knowledge to one of My prophets. Daniel was praying to seek knowledge about Israel's future, and I sent an angel with the answer."*

> "Then he said to me, 'Do not fear, Daniel, for from the first day that you set your heart to understand, and to humble yourself before your God, your words were heard; and I have come because of your words. But the prince of

the kingdom of Persia withstood me twenty-one days; and behold, Michael, one of the chief princes, came to help me, for I had been left alone there with the kings of Persia. Now I have come to make you understand what will happen to your people in the latter days, for the vision refers to many days yet to come'" (Daniel 10:12-14).

"Daniel was also shown mysteries about the end times and he was instructed to seal up this book.

There are secrets that I still want to reveal to My prophets in these last days. If My prophets will call to Me; I will answer them and show them great and mighty things from the record room. Draw near to Me, and I will draw near to you and whisper in your ear what I intend to accomplish in these last days. The identity of the Anti-Christ and the False Prophet are recorded, and when it is time, I will reveal them to My servants the prophets. Child, I showed you a glimpse of their faces when you were in Israel. The world will be shocked when they realize they have been deceived by these two men, but it will be too late. The book that I open up in the last days is also stored in the Record Room. This scroll contains the events of the last seven years before I return. It would be wise for people to study and glean from My Book of Revelation to get prepared. These events are real, and they will occur. My Word is Truth! My Word is established, and it is already done!"

Vows and oaths made to God are also recorded in the Record Room of heaven. "Hannah was barren and cried out to

God in desperation for a baby boy. Then she made a vow and said, 'O LORD of hosts, if You will indeed look on the affliction of Your maidservant and remember me, and not forget Your maidservant, but will give Your maidservant a male child, then I will give him to the LORD all the days of his life, and no razor shall come upon his head'" (1 Samuel 1:11). Although Hannah is the one that initiated the vow, it was the Spirit of God who prompted her to pledge her child to the Lord because God had a divine plan for Samuel.

When Samuel was weaned, Hannah kept her vow to God and dedicated him to work in the Temple. Like Hannah, God may allow you to experience a desperate situation so He can prompt you to make a commitment to Him. Through that commitment or vow, God's divine plans are fulfilled. When it is a Holy Spirit inspired vow, the promise that was offered to God will match perfectly with God's plans for your life. God takes vows very seriously, so if you have made a promise to submit to God and serve Him in any way; He will collect. "When you make a vow to the LORD your God, you shall not delay to pay it; for the LORD your God will surely require it of you" (Deuteronomy 23:21).

If there is ever a question that you took the vow or spoke the promise, God can go directly to the record room and provide the proof and send the Holy Spirit to remind you of it. The reminder of your promise to God could also come in the form of a dream, from the Word of God, or be spoken by the least expected person in your life. "If a man makes a vow to the LORD, or swears an oath to bind himself by some agreement, he shall not break his word; he shall do according to all that proceeds out of his mouth" (Numbers 30:1-2).

The Lord revealed to me there are other books in the Record Room, and one is called the Book of Creation. Every atom, molecular structure, and DNA strand is listed. The periodic tables of elements that man has discovered and named are just a partial list of the diverse elements of the universe. Every complex formula that comprises the law of physics, the laws of nature, gravitational laws, orbital laws, the laws of the earth, and the laws that govern the galaxies are documented in these volumes. The laws that govern the procreation of man, beast, bird, and fish are also documented. The formula for the division of human cells that begins at conception is in the Book of Creation. The complex molecular structure of the human brain is explained. The knowledge that man has achieved regarding the human body is just a fraction of what is contained in this great book.

Every part of the human body has been designed by the Master Creator, and the blueprint of the human anatomy is in the Book of Creation. God has given man the ability to gain knowledge about his own body, but there is much more to be discovered. All of creation and the mysteries surrounding it are recorded in these volumes of creation. The mystery of how God created the universe out of nothing and all knowledge of every aspect of creation is contained in the Book of Creation. There are numerous volumes that contain this vast amount of information!

Another book in the Record Room the Lord made known to me is called the Book of Diseases and Cures. Every disease known to mankind from the beginning of time is recorded with the symptoms and the progression of the disease. God has given man a natural cure for every sickness and disease, but man has chosen synthetic cures that are not as effective. The Lord said: *"I have given man herbs, plants, roots, bark, leaves, berries, fruits, vegetables, nuts, and oils as natural cures; but man has set them aside for his own ways. My cures are perfect for the human body, which I created, and there are no side effects. Every cure is recorded in the Book of Diseases and Cures."*

Many diseases that man currently battles with are a result of introducing synthetic substances into the body such as steroids, hormones, preservatives and other unnatural chemicals of which the human body was never designed to partake. Chemical fertilizers and pesticides in fruits and vegetables also contribute in breaking-down the human body when they are ingested. Doctors, pharmacists, and researchers would have all the knowledge of diseases and their cures with this book, but I wonder how many would use it today in place of their expensive drugs and costly surgical procedures!

The Book of the Law given to Moses, the Feasts of Israel, and the Covenants established by God are also recorded in books in the Record Room. The pattern for the tabernacle in the wilderness given to Moses and Solomon's Temple are also documented in volumes. God gave David all the dimensions and specifications for the temple, and Solomon was the one commissioned by God to build it. The blueprint for the third temple in Jerusalem is recorded in a book in the Record Room. This temple does not exist yet, but the details and dimensions were divinely given to Ezekiel by an angel that escorted him around this new temple. This record room is massive, but then again, everything about God and His heavenly abode speaks of His incomprehensible magnitude.

~ CHAPTER THIRTEEN ~

The Fellowship Room

I was worshipping the Lord, and I sensed very strongly in my spirit that there was another room in heaven that God wanted to show me. The Lord began to speak to me, and then He gave me a vision of this magnificent room in heaven called the Fellowship Room. I was escorted to a set of double doors that were ornately carved out of a dark, reddish wood. The doors were large and very thick, and the outside border of the door had a carved scroll design. The inner part of the door was recessed with beautiful carvings covering it. The door handles were long, ornate handles made from gold, and when the doors swung open, I was instantly captivated with the floor. It was like poured glass. Embedded under the glass were vibrant gemstones of every color that formed a magnificent pattern on the floor, and bright light from above caused these gemstones to come vibrantly alive.

The Lord told me that the various colored gemstones represented every tribe, every tongue and every nation. The cut of the stones were amazing. I have never seen precious stones cut into such unique shapes. Next, I looked up at the ceiling which was made of clear crystal, but there was a sparkle to it.

The ceiling was vaulted with many angled panels of crystals that met in a peak. I noticed that the room was circular, and the panels were placed to complete the circle. There was a bright beam of light shining through the crystal ceiling panels down to the floor that made the gems radiate their color.

The walls were also angled panels that formed a complete circle. On each of the wall panels were various carved scenes that depicted different eras throughout man's history. The first scene I saw was Adam and Even in the Garden of Eden. The scenes progressed through man's history around the circular room. Each scene was a carved three-dimensional depiction overlaid with pure gold. The detail was intricately superlative! When I gazed at the walls, they were so uniquely and artistically created, I felt like I was being drawn into that particular time in history. When I gazed around this room at this beautiful artwork, I realized the vast size of the Fellowship Room. The only thing I can compare its size to is a stadium.

Another scene that I saw was the Israelites at the Red Sea with the wall of water and the multitudes crossing over. I saw the tower-like beam of fire that separated the Israelites from Pharaoh's army. On one side of the tower of fire the Israelites were crossing over as Moses stood with His staff in his hand watching the people cross. On the other side were the chariots and the Egyptians with fear on their faces. The Holy Spirit revealed to me there were twenty-one scenes around this circular wall in the Fellowship Room that depicted the history of mankind in relationship to God. These are the scenes:

1. Adam and Eve in the Garden - God's Creation.
2. Noah and the Ark - God's Judgment.

3. Abraham about to sacrifice Isaac - God's Nation.
4. Moses at the burning bush - God's Appearance.
5. Crossing of the Red Sea- God's Deliverance.
6. Giving of the Law at Mount Sinai - God's Law.
7. Fall of Jericho and the entrance to the Promised Land - God's Promise.
8. David's coronation - God's King.
9. First Temple built by Solomon - God's Temple.
10. Elijah on Mt. Carmel - God's Fire.
11. Second Temple built by Zerubbabel - God's Cornerstone.
12. Gabriel announcing Jesus birth to Mary - God's Son.
13. Crucifixion of Jesus - God's Sacrifice.
14. Resurrection of Jesus - God's Glory.
15. Ascension of Jesus - God's Ascent.
16. Pentecost - God's Spirit.
17. Third Temple in Jerusalem - God's Design.
18. Jesus on white Horse with the saints - God's Battle.
19. Jesus planting His feet on the Mount of Olives - God's Return.
20. Thousand year reign of Jesus in Jerusalem - God's Reign.
21. New Jerusalem - God's Kingdom.

These scenes in the circular Fellowship Room depict the beginning to the end; from the Garden of Eden to the New Jerusalem. A completed circle! "And He said to me, 'It is done! I am the Alpha and the Omega, the Beginning and the End. I will give of the fountain of the water of life freely to him who thirsts. He who overcomes shall inherit all things, and I will be his God and he shall be My son'" (Revelation 21:6-7).

The Lord further explained about what happens in the Fellowship Room in heaven: *"Child, every time you proclaim the salvation message to a person, it is recorded in your book. The name of the person, the date and the place are all recorded. The Fellowship Room is the place where you will meet every person you ever gave the Gospel and also those you personally prayed with to receive Jesus as Savior. This room is elegant, opulent, and grand in every aspect. I designed this room for the purpose of reuniting people who were instrumental in bringing the Gospel to others. It is called the Fellowship Room for this reason.*

Child, you will be reunited with every person from every tribe and nation that you have touched with My Gospel message. This is one of your rewards for serving Me. I have blessings for those who serve Me, and I want to encourage you that these rewards await you. In the Fellowship Room there is every kind of musical instrument available to be played. The harp, piano, drums of various kinds, cellos, cymbals, trumpets, flutes, saxophones, harmonicas, tubas, violins, lyres, banjos, piccolos, trombones, xylophones, bells, and some heavenly instruments that you have never heard. Music is a great way to fellowship with one another. Whatever instrument you touch, you will be able to play, for nothing is impossible with God. There will be a lot of celebrating and gift giving. It will be like a birthday party in reverse.

The people celebrating their spiritual birthday will be giving gifts to the Gospel giver. It will be a time of great celebration and great joy! Invitations will be sent out for different parties. Everyone will have the opportunity to attend at least one fellowship party to honor the one who gave them the Gospel message. If they have brought others to Christ, then there will be a party thrown in their honor with all those attending who they have evangelized. Rewards are based on good works, and this is one of the rewards for preaching the Gospel. I want My children to know that I have rewards waiting for them so they do not grow weary in serving Me.

Each of the people that you have given the Gospel will present you with a precious gemstone and these jewels will be placed on your gown. When your jeweled gown is complete, you will wear it and be presented to Jesus as His bride. Each jewel on your gown represents a person in heaven that you evangelized by giving them the Gospel message. Child, I have shown you wearing your jeweled gown that had a long train to contain all your jewels. You will be presented to Jesus in this bejeweled gown."

This is the vision the Lord showed me: I saw myself in a long blue satin-like robe that had been draped over my shoulders. The garment was like a royal robe, but the color was light blue in color. It flowed from my shoulders to the floor and had a long train at the back. Underneath this cape-like royal robe, I had on a full-length, beautiful white gown; similar to a wedding gown. The gown was covered with small gemstones from the bodice to the long train. I felt like royalty in this shimmering white, gem-studded gown. Upon my head was a beautiful tiara covered with brilliant diamonds and rubies. My outward appearance was this: I had long wavy tresses of hair the color of spun gold. My eyes were a vibrant green that had shimmering flecks of gold that danced in the light. My skin was a creamy peach, and my complexion was perfect. My lips were a soft pink, and my teeth a pearly white that gleamed when I smiled. I have never felt or looked as beautiful as I did in this vision, and I was greatly rejoicing just like Isaiah when he said:

> "I will greatly rejoice in the LORD, My soul
> shall be joyful in my God;
> For He has clothed me with the
> garments of salvation,
> He has covered me with the robe of
> righteousness,
> As a bridegroom decks himself with
> ornaments,
> And as a bride adorns herself with her jewels"
> (Isaiah 49:18).

This time of celebration in the Fellowship Room will be filled with such a mixture of emotions. There will be joyful laughter as we bask in the sweet ambiance of being connected to one another through Christ. There will be intense gratitude for the one who gave you the Gospel and even more gratitude for the One who is the Giver of the Gospel. It will be a festive time with singing and playing musical instruments. There will be delicious food and wonderful reminiscing. There will be introductions from the ones as they remind you of the time and place you shared the Gospel with them. It will be a glorious time! After all the reminiscing, after all the introductions, and after all the gift giving, the Lord of Lords and King of Kings will make a grand entrance to your party.

His eyes will radiate pure love and joy at this great reunion of the children of God that only His Father could have orchestrated. All of the attention that was being given to you as the guest of honor will now be focused on Jesus! As Jesus winds His way through the crowd of people, He will not take His eyes from you. The King of Glory has come to your party to thank you for taking His message to these people surrounding you. Amazing! There is such an intense love emanating from His eyes as He gazes into yours. This moment becomes an entire lifetime wrapped up in His loving eyes as you are forever drawn into the depths of His captivating gaze. You excitedly show Him your cache of jewels that will be placed on your gown, and He smiles with sweet delight and says, "Well done My good and faithful servant." You have waited a lifetime to hear those words, and they are the perfect climax to your heavenly party in the Fellowship Room!

~ CHAPTER FOURTEEN ~

The Prayer Room

When Jesus taught the disciples to pray, He said, "Our Father in heaven. Hallowed be thy name. Thy kingdom come. Thy will be done. As in heaven so on earth (Matthew 6:9-10 AENT)." This is the correct order of the words in this prayer according to the literal Aramaic English translation of the Bible. God is a God of order, and when Jesus said, "Thy will be done in heaven so on earth," it reveals God's order of creation and His order for His will. Everything proceeded forth from heaven from the Father, starting with the creation of the world. The pattern for everything that God has planned for us has its beginning in heaven because man was patterned after the image of God. The earthly tabernacle that was given to Moses was also patterned after the heavenly tabernacle, and this is important regarding our prayer and worship.

In the tabernacle there was the outer court, the Most Holy Place, and the Holy of Holies. The Holy of Holies contained the Ark of the Covenant, and the high priest would go in once a year, on the Day of Atonement, and sprinkle the blood of animals. In the Most Holy Place, the articles included a golden censer, a golden altar, a golden lamp stand, and a golden table for the showbread. It is important to recognize God's order in the tabernacle so one can understand that prayer was first established in heaven.

The altar of incense in the Old Testament tabernacle was a type of worship that would foreshadow the true worship of the church. "You shall make an altar to burn incense on; you shall make it of acacia wood. Aaron shall burn on it sweet incense every morning; when he tends the lamps, he shall burn incense on it. And when Aaron lights the lamps at twilight, he shall burn incense on it, a perpetual incense before the LORD throughout your generations" (Exodus 30:1, 7, 8).

When Aaron and the high priests burnt incense on the altar, the aroma rose to the throne of God as an act of worship, and this foreshadowed the individual and corporate worship that would be mixed with the incense and rise to the throne of God. God also warned the Israelites that if sin abounded in their lives, then the Lord would not smell or acknowledge their burnt offering of worship on the altar of incense. "And after all this, if you do not obey Me, but walk contrary to Me, then I also will walk contrary to you in fury; and I, even I, will chastise you seven times for your sins. I will lay your cities waste and bring your sanctuaries to desolation, and I will not smell the fragrance of your sweet aromas" (Leviticus 26:27-28, 31).

We need to realize that if sin abounds in our lives because there is no repentance, then God will not smell the sweet fragrance of our worship. Jesus addressed this issue when He said, "These people draw near to Me with their mouth, And honor Me with their lips, But their heart is far from Me" (Matthew 15:8). The Lord also spoke these words to me regarding worship: *"There are gates of prayer and worship which are either open or closed depending upon the hearts of people. If My people continue in sin, then the gates are closed, and I do not receive their worship mixed with incense rising as a sweet aroma. If My people have pure hearts and clean hands, then the gates of worship are open, and I will smell the sweet aroma of their worship. Sin is crouching at the door and is ready to take possession of the gates of prayer and worship. I warned Cain that sin was about to overtake him, but he did not heed My warning, and he killed his brother Abel. The first murder was the result of wrong worship because Cain's heart was not right before Me. Cain wanted to worship his way instead of My way. Obedience is better than sacrifice. The gates of worship for Cain were closed because of his disobedience, and after he killed his brother, the gates of worship were forever closed because My presence was no longer with him."*

A scripture in Revelation paints a very vivid picture about how prayer works in the heavenly realm. The Lord opened up my understanding of earthly and heavenly prayer in a way that has transformed my theology on prayer and has given me a fresh appreciation and excitement for prayer.

> "When He opened the seventh seal, there was silence in heaven for about half an hour. And I saw the seven angels who stand before God, and to them were given seven trumpets. Then another angel, having a golden censer, came and stood at the altar. He was given much incense, that he should offer it with the

prayers of all the saints upon the golden altar which was before the throne. And the smoke of the incense, with the prayers of the saints, ascended before God from the angel's hand" (Revelation 8:1-4).

When Jesus opens the seventh seal there will be complete silence in heaven. There will be no activity, no praising, no singing, no movement; just eerie silence. All of heaven will be holding their breath anticipating the dramatic event that is about to unfold on earth. When the seventh seal has been opened, the contents will be a horrific judgment on the inhabitants of the earth. Immediately, an angel will have a golden censer ready to burn incense mixed with the prayers of the saints. The smoke of the incense will rise to the throne of God along with these prayers.

The question arises concerning where these prayers originated, since all the saints have been either martyred or taken up to heaven in the catching away of the church. The Lord gave me His answer when He said: *"I want to show you the Prayer Room in heaven. Allow Me to unfold this room to your spirit in a way that will transform your prayers. First, you cannot separate prayer from worship. The church on earth has compartmentalized and separated prayer and worship as if they are different entities. They are the same. When you worship Me, you are praying, and when you pray, you are worshipping Me. Patricia, you have experienced the oneness of prayer and worship, and you never realized they were one. Often when you are worshipping Me in song, you begin to pray in the Spirit. When you worship, you are praying, and when you are praying you are worshipping; they are not separate.*

Prayer and worship is the same in heaven. My children gather together in a Prayer Room in heaven. There is a call to prayer, and an angel sounds a trumpet in heaven to summon my children to pray and worship. These prayers are collected by the angels in heaven and mixed with the incense, and they rise to My throne. Now that you understand the Prayer Room in heaven, I want to give you a glimpse of what happens there."

This is what the Lord showed me about this heavenly room called the Prayer Room. It was a tall tower, about three stories high with glass-like walls. The walls were not smooth. They had small cut rectangular panels that had a unique ability to refract light which created a rainbow of color. It was almost as if the walls were made of a multitude of prisms molded together into one piece. The vibrant colors were very beautiful.

Standing in the middle of the room gave me the sense I was standing in the center of a very elegant crystal chandelier, and the light was shimmering through the cut crystal. The floor was a pure transparent gold that reflected the vibrant colors coming from the crystal walls. There was a multitude of musical instruments just as there was in the Fellowship Room.

The construction of this room was such that it was acoustically perfect in every aspect. It was acoustically perfect for a choir, an acapella voice, or with full instrumentation. The Holy Spirit revealed to me there is not just one Prayer Room; there are a many situated throughout heaven. Just as the Levites had a schedule for temple duty, there is a schedule for the rotation of people to participate in the activities in the Prayer Room in heaven. The Holy Spirit showed me one of the activities that occur in the Prayer Room.

Angels gather the prayers of God's children on earth, and they record them in a book in the Record Room. There are many prayers that are so intense that tears accompany them. "You number my wanderings; Put my tears into Your bottle; Are they not in Your book? When I cry out to You, Then my enemies will turn back; This I know, because God is for me" (Psalm 57:7-9). Our prayers on earth that are birthed by the Holy Spirit are shared with those in heaven. Those in the Prayer Room in heaven pray in agreement with our prayers on earth, and they are lifted to the throne of God. It becomes a unity of spirit with the saints in heaven and the saints on earth.

In the Book of Hebrews, there is a list of patriarchs that were a great cloud of witnesses that went to heaven without ever having received the promise on earth. These patriarchs join with us in prayer in heaven as we lift our prayers to God the Father! This joining of prayers of the Old Testament saints and the New Testament saints bring a fresh meaning to these verses describing the faithful patriarchs. "And all these, having obtained a good testimony through faith, did not receive the promise, God having provided something better for us, that they should not be made perfect apart from us" (Hebrews 11:39-40).

Although the Old Testament saints never saw the fulfillment of God's promise while they were on earth, the fulfillment of God's promise has been made complete through Jesus Christ with the joining of the redeemed saints in heaven and on earth. The Holy Spirit explained how our prayers on earth reach those in heaven so there is a unity of Spirit regarding prayer: *"The saints in heaven play a vital role in the kingdom. Many of them never saw the promise fulfilled when they lived on earth, but they are witnesses to the promises being fulfilled while they are in heaven. Child, I send My angels to earth to record prayers and events that are happening in the world, and they bring back a report to those in heaven. Those in heaven, whom I have chosen, receive these reports so they can pray and worship."* It is important to remember that we should always pray to our heavenly Father and Jesus and not to the saints in heaven. Prayer is an essential benchmark in God's structure of heaven and earth. In order to understand fully how our prayers work to release God's power, the Lord showed me a triangle which I call the Prayer Triangle.

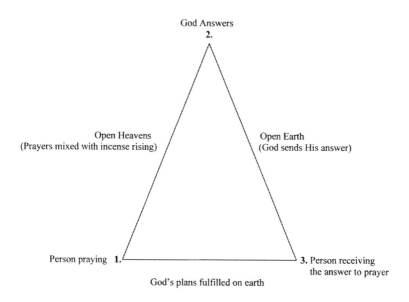

The Prayer Triangle is beautifully illustrated in this story in scripture.

> "Peter was therefore kept in prison, but constant prayer was offered to God for him by the church. And when Herod was about to bring him out, that night Peter was sleeping, bound with two chains between two soldiers; and the guards before the door were keeping the prison. Now behold, an angel of the Lord stood by him, and a light shone in the prison; and he struck Peter on the side and raised him up, saying, 'Arise quickly!' And his chains fell off his hands. Then the angel said to him, 'Gird yourself and tie on your sandals'; and so he did. And he said to him, 'Put on your garment and follow me.' So he went out and followed him, and did not know that what was done by the angel was real, but thought he was seeing a vision. When they were past the first and the second guard posts, they came to the iron gate that leads to the city, which opened to them of its own accord; and they went out and went down one street, and immediately the angel departed from him. And when Peter had come to himself, he said, 'Now I know for certain that the Lord has sent His angel, and has delivered me from the hand of Herod and from all the expectation of the Jewish people.' So, when he had considered this, he came to the house of Mary, the mother of John whose surname was

Mark, where many were gathered together praying" (Acts 12:5-13).

Looking at the prayer triangle, first the church was praying for Peter who was put in prison. They had come together in Mary's home, and with a unity of spirit, they asked God for Peter's release. This was a perilous time for the followers of Jesus Christ because the Apostles and disciples were being put to death. The church had gathered with a fervency and desperation as they cried out to God on behalf of Peter. The heavens were opened, and the prayers were mixed with the incense and rose to the throne of God.

God knew exactly what was happening with Peter, yet He did not act until the prayers of the saints rose to His throne. This reveals the importance of prayer! Our Father in heaven wants us to present our petitions and requests to Him so we learn to depend upon Him. God heard the prayers mixed with the sweet aroma of the incense as the saints were interceding for Peter, and He sent an angel down to earth who miraculously broke Peter out of jail. Peter was the recipient of the answered prayer, and God's plans were fulfilled on earth.

The prayer triangle was completed when Peter showed up at Mary's house from where the prayer and worship was being lifted. The amazing part of the story happens when Peter knocked on the door of Mary's house and those praying did not believe he was actually there. The early church had not yet grasped the power of their prayer to change the outcome of Peter's destiny. I wonder if the church today realizes they have the power to change the destiny of people lives through prayer.

Through prayer, we also have the power to change our own destiny as we lift our daily requests to the Lord. God deeply yearns to hear from His children about every detail of their lives. The Lord's very tenderly spoke these words to me: *"I desire to hear from My children through prayer and worship. Please know that this is a two-way communication. If My people will draw close to Me through prayer and worship, then I will draw near to them, and they will hear My voice. I deeply desire to talk with My children. True Prayer and worship keeps one humble because they are acknowledging I am God, and I am all-powerful, all-knowing, and ever-present. Now I want to show you in the Spirit what happens as people pray and worship Me in spirit and truth."*

I saw myself in this vision, and I was singing, worshipping, and dancing before the Lord. There were twelve angels surrounding me, and they were facing away from me in a circle as a ring of protection. Then I saw a different angel above me, and he was collecting my praise and worship in golden bowls and mixing it with incense. The incense rose to the throne of God, and the Holy Spirit revealed to me that everyone's worship has a distinct aroma. God the Father recognized my scent of worship and spoke this to me in the vision: *"Ah, Patricia is praising Me!"* The Lord also spoke these words to me regarding worship: *"When you corporately worship, all the worship is collected in these golden bowls and is mixed with incense and rises to My throne. I can identify each church's worship by their unique aroma that rises up."*

It is important that we pray and worship because God

gave man dominion over the earth, and we release God to act on earth through our prayers and worship. Although God is sovereign and He can do whatever He chooses on earth; He has chosen to relinquish some of His power to mankind by giving us dominion over the earth. When we pray in God's will, heavenly things occur on earth that God wants to happen. If we do not pray, then those things remain undone in the earthly realm. Our prayers, supplication and worship are mixed with incense and collected in golden bowls by the angels and ascend to God's throne. In God's perfect timing, he sends forth His answer to earth so His plans are fulfilled.

God desires us to pray and worship so His kingdom will be established on earth as it is in heaven. You cannot help but see that the world around us is changing very rapidly just as Jesus predicted it would happen. I truly believe that we are entering into the last years, and God is calling forth His prayer warriors and worshippers to release His will in these perilous times. Prophetic worship is one such ministry that God is establishing in these last days. In order to understand the ministry of prophetic worship for today, we must examine the biblical pattern established by God.

> "Moreover David and the captains of the army separated for the service some of the sons of Asaph, of Heman, and of Jeduthun, who should prophesy with harps, stringed instruments, and cymbals. Asaph, Jeduthun, and Heman were under the authority of the king. So the number of them, with their brethren who were instructed in the songs of the LORD, all who

were skillful, was two hundred and eighty-eight. Now the first lot for Asaph came out for Joseph; the second for Gedaliah, him with his brethren and sons, twelve; the third for Zaccur, his sons and his brethren, twelve... the twenty-third for Mahazioth, his sons and his brethren, twelve; the twenty-fourth for Romamti-Ezer, his sons and his brethren, twelve" (1Chronicles 25:1, 7, 9, 10, 31).

The number of prophetic worshippers was significant in this scripture. There were twelve worshippers in each group, and there were twenty-four groups of twelve. Twelve is the number of divine government and apostolic fullness while twenty-four is the number of priestly governmental perfection. Not all the Levites who praised the Lord were prophetic worshippers. "Of these, twenty-four thousand were to look after the work of the house of the LORD, six thousand were officers and judges, four thousand were gatekeepers, and four thousand praised the LORD with musical instruments, 'which I made,' said David, 'for giving praise'" (1Chronicles 23:4-5). There were four thousand who praised the Lord with musical instruments, but only two hundred and eighty-eight were set apart to prophesy with musical instruments and songs.

According to this scripture, there were four key aspects to prophetic worship. First, a prophetic worshipper must be sanctified for this ministry, and everyone who was set apart had a duty. The Lord spoke these words to me regarding this ministry: ***"I am the One who sets apart an individual for prophetic worship. The ministry requires a very close*** *walk with Me. Your intimate relationship with Me through the prophetic ministry is not to be taken lightly. There is much power in prophetic worship. Battles are won in the spiritual realm as a result of true prophetic worship. Chains of bondages are broken for salvation, healing and deliverance.*

Through worship, people will be prepared to receive the gospel, their physical bodies will be healed, emotional trauma will be lifted, and they will be delivered from the demonic. Through prophetic worship, the gates of the enemy will be possessed, and the land will be set free from demonic oppression. I send My prophetic worshippers into the land to worship with songs and with musical instruments to release My power for proclaiming the gospel. There are several ways a person is called into prophetic worship. The calling can come directly from the Holy Spirit, the calling can be announced by one of My prophets, or the calling is obtained when a person's spirit bears witness that they have been given an anointing for worship that has been sanctified by God. A person will know they are called into prophetic worship when their worship produces results, and they notice people getting saved, healed, and delivered."

The second aspect of prophetic worship was they gave thanks and praise to the Lord with musical instruments. This was not an ordinary playing of musical instruments because they prophesied with harps and stringed instruments. These Levites were also instructed in the songs of the Lord. The Lord spoke this: *"Prophetic worship is done with musical instruments and the voice. Some are gifted with both musical instruments and voice while some are gifted in instruments only or voice only. Both are very powerful weapons in battling the spiritual realm. A song that glorifies, praises, and worships God can be sung or played in prophetic worship. Singing Alleluia is a powerful way to worship."*

Alleluia is an adoring exclamation that comes from two Hebrew words, *Halal* and *Yahh.* The Hebrew form of Alleluia is Hallelujah. *Halal* means "to shine, to boast, to celebrate, and to sing; to be worthy of praise." *Yahh* is the sacred name of God and means the Lord most vehement. By singing this simple yet powerful refrain to the Lord, the worshipper is announcing that only God is worthy of praise!

"Singing Psalms and scripture releases My power. Singing in tongues is also a very powerful way to worship because the songs will well up in your spirit by the leading of the Holy Spirit. Some songs that are sung in prophetic worship are previously learned songs, and some are new songs. This new song is one that you have never learned before because it is a song given to you by the Holy Spirit. It can also be a song that you have never played before on your musical instrument. The Holy Spirit will inspire you to play this new song. The singing and playing of musical instruments are inspired by the Holy Spirit and can be of a predictive nature or a simple discourse."

The third characteristic of the prophetic worshipper is they were under the authority of the king, according to the order of the king. Worship was done orderly and at specific times and locations. All prophetic worshippers must be under the authority of the Lord of lords and King of kings, Jesus

Christ. God has set up a chain of spiritual authority in His Word. "But I want you to know that the head of every man is Christ, the head of woman is man, and the head of Christ is God" (1Corinthians 11:3). God the Father is the head of Christ, Christ is the head of every man, and man is the head of the woman. Those who are prophetic worshippers must be under the proper authority and submit to their God given authority. The man must fully submit to Christ and the woman must fully submit to the man God has given her as a spiritual covering. If there is a lack of submission by the man or the woman, then they are open for an attack of the enemy. Since worship is a weapon of spiritual warfare, it is imperative that the worshipper has the full protection of God. The full protection can only be in effect when obedience to God's chain of authority is followed.

The fourth component of a prophetic worshipper was some were seers in the words of God. A seer is one who beholds visions and is also a prophet. Not all the prophetic worshippers were seers or prophets. Only fourteen of the two hundred and eighty-eight were seers, so this was an elite group chosen by God. God gave them visions to instruct them, to guide and protect them, and to reveal His plans. "Surely the Lord GOD does nothing, Unless He reveals His secret to His servants the prophets" (Amos 3:7).

In order to appreciate more fully why God chose musical instruments and songs for prophetic worship, the creation of worship must be understood. Lucifer was a cherub who was created by God to worship Him.

"You were the seal of perfection,
Full of wisdom and perfect in beauty.

You were in Eden, the garden of God;
Every precious stone was your covering:
The sardius, topaz, and diamond,
Beryl, onyx, and jasper,
Sapphire, turquoise, and emerald with gold.
The workmanship of your timbrels and pipes
Was prepared for you on the day you were
created.
You were the anointed cherub who covers"
(Ezekiel 28:12-14).

When Lucifer rebelled against God and was cast down from the mountain of God, he became Satan. The very one who was created by God to worship is the very one who placed people in the bondage of spiritual death, sin and sickness. Lucifer's worship became corrupted, but God intervened and created man to worship Him. When Satan deceived Eve and Adam and they both sinned, God's plan for pure worship was once again thwarted. But God still had a plan to perfect worship so it would once again be pure and undefiled. His plan continued when Jubal became the father of all those who would play musical instruments. "His brother's name was Jubal. He was the father of all those who play the harp and flute" (Genesis 4:21).

Worship through musical instruments was now introduced to man, where before it was for the angelic realm. Next, the year of Jubilee was introduced to the Levites by God. Every fifty years all the slaves were set free and all debts were forgiven. This year of Jubilee was a year of liberty and freedom for the people. The connection between Jubal's name and the year of Jubilee was not just in name only. Jubal, who was the father of all who worshipped through musical instruments and the fiftieth year of Jubilee, had a much deeper spiritual connection. The playing of musical instruments in prophetic worship would set people free from bondages, sickness and oppression because it was a year of Jubilee!

When God redeemed man through Jesus Christ His Son, He also redeemed the corrupted worship that came as the result of the fall of Satan and the fall of man. The Levites were set apart to be prophetic worshippers, and through their worship, they were preparing for the Messiah to come. Prophesying through musical instruments and voices lifted in praise was God's plan to usher in Jesus Christ. The Levites did not fully understand the great power of their ministry, but King David knew the importance of prophetic worship to usher in the Messiah.

Many of David's Psalms were accompanied by musical instruments and sung. Psalms Two, Twenty, and Twenty-Two were prophetic in their predictions of the coming of the Messiah. David also understood the power of worship for deliverance from his enemies. Some of the most intense spiritual warfare Psalms were written and sung by David when he was running from Saul. An in-depth study of the Psalms will reveal that King David was God's greatest prophetic worshipper of all time. It is no wonder that God is calling His people to rebuild the tabernacle of David to restore David's house of praise and worship! The Holy Spirit of God is calling His true worshippers to prophesy through worship in these last days to usher in the Second Coming of Jesus!

Prophetic worship is a powerful tool for the salvation

of souls. The Holy Spirit showed me firsthand the power of prophetic worship while I was in India. I was staying with a pastor and his wife that are very dear to me, and their maid would come in the mornings to clean their house. I was worshipping the Lord when she came to clean, and the natural inclination was to stop singing, but the Spirit of God told me to continue worshipping. The next morning, I had a dream. There was a maidservant washing clothes in a bucket and hanging them on the line on the pastor's patio. This maid beckoned to me in the dream and said she was ready to receive Jesus as her Lord. The morning I had the dream, the maid came once again to clean the pastor's home. She had heard the Gospel many times from the pastor, and he would lovingly tease her that when the Rapture comes she will not have to clean the house because they will all be gone. She consistently refused Jesus as her Savior, but this morning was different. She asked me to pray with her, and I sensed she was ready to receive Jesus which lined-up with the dream I was given by the Holy Spirit. While I was praying with her for her salvation, the Holy Spirit clearly spoke to me and said it was my prophetic worship that she heard that broke through the final barrier for her salvation. The worship spoke to her spirit that she needed a Savior and carried a powerful anointing to break through the bondage of the enemy.

David, who was a great worshipper, knew the anointing of his worship to breakthrough his enemies. "So David went to Baal Perazim, and David defeated them there; and he said, 'The LORD has broken through my enemies before me, like a breakthrough of water.' Therefore he called the name of that place Baal Perazim" (2 Samuel 5:20). Baal Perazim literally means "Master of breakthroughs." By worshipping the Master, there is a breakthrough from the oppression of the enemy that enables people to be set free from sin and to become born again by the Spirit of God.

Prophetic worship is also a spiritual weapon for deliverance of people who are possessed or oppressed by Satan and his demons. While I was in South Africa, the power of prophetic worship to set captives free was displayed magnificently. I was attending a special Christian service held on their Election Day in a poor, black township of Soweto. At the end of the message, the pastor had an altar call, and people began to fill the two aisles in this large circus size tent. A very violent woman came up the aisle escorted by two burly ushers, and I immediately knew she was demon possessed. She had an unnatural strength, and the two ushers had difficulty keeping her constrained. She tried to bite and kick the ushers, and she spit in my face when I was ministering to her and telling her that Jesus loved her.

I continued to pray in tongues, and the demonic spirit within her was very agitated with my prayers. With a guttural voice of the demon she snarled at me, "I hate you!" She broke loose from the ushers leaping towards me with a look of murder in her eyes. The ushers grabbed her and pinned her to the floor to restrain her from any violent act. The breakthrough came when the pastor began quietly singing worship songs as she ministered to the woman, and I continued to pray in tongues. I witnessed a phenomenal transformation as this woman was being set free from the evil spirit that possessed her. The worship sank deep within her spirit to set her free, and this aggressive woman who wanted to kill me just moments earlier was sitting docile and calm and saying that she loved Jesus. It was truly amazing to see this violent demon possessed woman who was being groomed to be a witchdoctor transformed into this beautiful, gentle child of God through the power of prophetic worship and prayer. At the end of the service I wrapped my arms around her in a big bear hug, kissed her cheek and told her that I loved her. We both had tears welling up in our eyes knowing that we were sisters in Christ for all eternity. The power of prayer and worship was extraordinary and supernatural that day in South Africa, and we need to be keenly aware of the power God has given us. Prayer and worship are so vital that it continues in the Prayer Room in heaven until all of God's plans are fulfilled.

CHAPTER FIFTEEN

The Throne Room

The most vivid description that we have of the throne room in heaven is in the Book of Revelation. The Apostle John was taken up to heaven in the Spirit and was shown this marvelous phenomenon of God's throne.

> "After these things I looked, and behold, a door standing open in heaven. And the first voice which I heard was like a trumpet speaking with me, saying, 'Come up here, and I will show you things which must take place after this.' Immediately I was in the Spirit; and behold, a throne set in heaven, and One sat on the throne. And He who sat there was like a jasper and a sardius stone in appearance; and there was a rainbow around the throne, in appearance like an emerald. Around the throne were twenty-four thrones, and on the thrones I saw twenty-four elders sitting, clothed in white robes; and they had crowns of gold on their heads. And from the throne proceeded lightnings,

thunderings, and voices. Seven lamps of fire were burning before the throne, which are the seven Spirits of God" (Revelation 4:1-5).

John saw a throne, and he described God sitting on the throne having the appearance of jasper and sardius which are precious stones that are crimson red and golden yellow in color, much like the color of flames. The vibrant rainbow that he observed was the glory of God brilliantly encasing the throne like a circular cover of magnificent splendor. He could observe God's royal throne through the iridescent rainbow just like viewing a translucent emerald held up to a light. He could see the beauty of God on His throne through the impressive splash of color. Ezekiel was also given a vision of God's throne, and what he viewed was very similar to what John saw.

"And above the firmament over their heads was the likeness of a throne, in appearance like a sapphire stone; on the likeness of the throne was a likeness with the appearance of a man high above it. Also from the appearance of His waist and upward I saw, as it were, the color of amber with the appearance of fire all around within it; and from the appearance of His waist and downward I saw, as it were, the appearance of fire with brightness all around. Like the appearance of a rainbow in a cloud on a rainy day, so was the appearance of the brightness all around it. This was the appearance of the likeness of the glory of the LORD" (Ezekiel 1:26-28).

Ezekiel included a different detail of the throne when he described it as having the appearance of a sapphire stone. Sapphires are a vibrant blue, the color often worn by royalty. He equated the appearance of God like fire all around, the same way that Moses encountered God on Mount Sinai. Ezekiel described the rainbow around the throne of God, and the Lord showed me in the Spirit how this rainbow surrounds His throne. Most often when we think of a rainbow, we picture an arc because that is how we see rainbows in nature. The rainbow that I saw in the Spirit was different because it was a circular rainbow encircling the throne. With the throne in the center, this shimmering rainbow was rotating around it like the rings that rotate around Saturn.

It was an awesome sight to view these sparkling vibrant colors dancing like pieces of tinted glitter floating on a beam of sunshine. The only rainbow I have ever viewed that even came close to this magnificent rainbow encircling the throne, was a double rainbow in California. A film maker took me to a winery that was situated at the top of a three hundred foot knoll with a spectacular view of the Napa Valley. It was raining lightly, and when the sun broke through, a brilliant double rainbow swept across the horizon. At that moment I knew I was experiencing a special gift from God. It wasn't until the Lord gave me the vision of the rainbow around His throne that I fully understood the California rainbow. God was giving me a glimpse of His glory in the double rainbow; the same glory that emanates from His throne.

Absorbing this breathtaking view of God's throne, John noticed there were twenty-four less ostentatious thrones encircling this splendid throne. Men clothed in white robes with gold crowns sat on these thrones. Then suddenly, his attention was abruptly ripped away from the twenty-four elders when flashes of lightening and claps of thunder erupted from the throne. It was almost as if God was saying, "Take your eyes from those twenty-four elders and focus on Me!" How often do we get distracted by people and events, and we take our focus from God? The Lord waits and waits for us to turn to Him instead of relying on everyone else's advice. God desires to break our stubborn independence so we call upon Him first when trials of life present themselves. The seven Spirits of God that are before the throne help us through all of life's challenges if we choose to call upon the Lord. They are identified by Isaiah as the Spirit of the Lord, the Spirit of wisdom, the Spirit of understanding, the Spirit of counsel, the Spirit of might, the Spirit of knowledge, and the Spirit of the fear of the Lord.

Around the throne, John witnessed these bizarre looking creatures that had an extraordinary task assigned to them. These peculiar four faced living beings with six wings and a multitude of eyes ceaselessly proclaimed God's holiness and power. They were always in the presence of God; never leaving their position, nor failing to give Him glory and honor.

"Before the throne there was a sea of glass, like crystal. And in the midst of the throne, and around the throne, were four living creatures full of eyes in front and in back. The first living creature was like a lion, the second living creature like a calf, the third living creature had a face like a man, and the fourth living creature was like a flying eagle. The four living creatures, each having six wings, were full of eyes around and within. And they do not rest day or night, saying: 'Holy, holy, holy, Lord God Almighty, Who was and is and is to come!' Whenever the living creatures give glory and honor and thanks to Him who sits on the throne, who lives forever and ever, the twenty-four elders fall down before Him who sits on the throne and worship Him who lives forever and ever, and cast their crowns before the throne, saying: 'You are worthy, O Lord, To receive glory and honor and power; For You created all things, And by Your will they exist and were created'" (Revelation 4: 6-11).

Another compelling fact is that this scripture mentions only four of these living creatures associated with God's throne. The Lord revealed the significance of the four living creatures and their four faces: ***"The number four in Scripture signifies holiness unto the Lord and also is the number associated with creation. The four living creatures are holy unto Me and their four faces represent My creation. When they worship Me, all of My creation is worshipping Me. The birds of the air, the beasts of the field, the animals of burden, and the men of the earth are worshipping Me through the living creatures when they cry out: "Holy, Holy, Holy, Lord God Almighty!" My creation worships Me in ways that man is not aware. The stars bow down, and it appears on earth as a twinkling star. The moon stays in its circular orbit as an*** *act of obedience and worship. The sun rises every day in the east in honor of Me, it's Creator. The wind, the rain, and the snow obey My voice. The animals of the forest honor Me by only procreating with their own species. The flowers open their petals in worship and send up their sweet fragrance to My nostrils. All of My creation worships Me!"*

"Praise the LORD!
Praise the LORD from the heavens;
Praise Him in the heights!
Praise Him, all His angels;
Praise Him, all His hosts!
Praise Him, sun and moon;
Praise Him, all you stars of light!
Praise Him, you heavens of heavens,
And you waters above the heavens!
Let them praise the name of the LORD,
For He commanded and they were created.
He also established them forever and ever;
He made a decree which shall not pass away.
Praise the LORD from the earth,
You great sea creatures and all the depths;
Fire and hail, snow and clouds;
Stormy wind, fulfilling His word;"
(Psalm 48:1-8).

The sanctity of God's creation has been set aside by man through human reasoning and scientific calculations. God is the Creator of the universe, and it did not exist before He created it. Even renowned physicists understand that quantum creation is the "tunneling" of the universe from nothing and its eternal inflation. They know the initial state of the universe never existed. It was pure nothingness without dimension, space, time, energy or content.

The missing link that physicists fail to understand in quantum creation is the God factor. The energy needed for the galaxies to come into existence from purely nothing is enormously greater than can be calculated through scientific equations. The power that was needed for the creation of the universe can only come from God. There is no other scientific explanation that will ever appease this fantastic phenomenon called quantum creation. No matter how high the level of his intelligence, man cannot possibly wrap his finite mind around an infinite God. We need to realize that our individual intelligence level is a gift from God through His divine impartation when our cells were first being formed. "For You formed my inward parts; You covered me in my mother's womb. I will praise You, for I am fearfully and wonderfully made" (Psalm 139:13-14).

Acknowledging that your intelligence is a gift from God removes any possible boasting and prevents you from disparaging others who may be less intelligent. Pride says: "Look at how intelligent I am. Look at my degrees. Look at how many languages I can speak. Look at my social status because I am an intellect." God reminds us that we all have a limited knowledge, and the extent of knowledge we do possess comes from Him. "'For My thoughts are not your thoughts, Nor are your ways My ways,' says the LORD. ' For as the heavens are higher than the earth, So are My ways higher than your ways, And My thoughts than your thoughts'" (Isaiah 55:8-9). We have all been created by God, and each person is only a small thread in this grand tapestry of the universe that He is intricately weaving.

As I conversed with the Lord Most High, He spoke to me about how His creation of the universe is intricately linked to man's worship: *"Child I have created other galaxies, but I chose the earth to create man. I formed man in My image, and he has a unique relationship to Me. Even the angels that I created are not in My likeness. Man's physical body is limited to time and space, but man's spirit transcends time and space. The spirit of man can travel to other dimensions such as heaven or hell or other galaxies, but his body remains on earth. When I show you things in the spirit, your body remains on earth, but your spirit sees things that are in different realms. John's spirit was taken to heaven where I showed him marvelous events. There is no time in eternity, and that is why a day is as a thousand years, and a thousand years is as a day."*

"Lord, I asked, "At what point in this vast universe does time cease to exist?"

"Time is created by the earth's rotation around the sun. I created time when I created the earth, the sun and the moon. I established what a day would be, what a week would be, what a month would be, and what a year would be. I created the seasons. Time is My creation. When you leave the earth's atmosphere, time ceases to exist. That is the reason there is no aging in eternity, because there is no time. The flowers never wither. Their colors are magnificent! There are colors and hues in heaven that man has never witnessed on earth. The grass is always perfect, and the trees never lose their leaves. Nothing decays in

heaven because there is no time. I want to show you the meadows, the fields, the flowers and the trees in heaven. I know how much you love the outdoors and the flowers, and I want to give you a glimpse of these in heaven."

In this vision I saw myself standing on a grassy hill, my hands were above my head, and I was twirling around. There was a sense of complete freedom in my spirit. There were no burdens or worries, and I felt light with joy. Standing on this plush hill, which felt like velvet on my feet, I could see there were a lot of beautiful meadows and hills where one could be alone. This appealed greatly to me because I enjoy quiet solitude in the beautiful outdoors. I could see an entire meadow of vibrant flowers as far as my eyes could see. It was an extraordinary sight.

I saw one flower that had unusual shaped purple petals on the exterior, the interior petals were aqua blue, and the center was a bright yellow. I could see diverse species of flowers that were red, pink, yellow, orange, fuchsia, blue, lime green; the colors were electric. The magnificent variety of flowers which I had never seen before were endless. It was so amazing! It was a horticulturists dream, and in my case, a gardeners dream to see such an array of flowers all flourishing in this meadow.

I also saw an unusual tree that looked like a combination of an African acacia and a weeping willow. This tree was spectacular as its branches formed a large umbrella with its long flowing branches that canopied over a grassy knoll. It was the perfect place to recline in quiet solitude and bask in the presence of the Lord.

"Lord God, You choose to reside in man after they are

born again by Your Spirit. How does an infinite God reside in the body of a man who is finite?"

"Child, I do not reside in the body of man. I reside in the spirit of man which has no constraints on time and space. Your body constrains you to this earth; but your spirit is free to move."

"Please explain how our spirits are free to move."

"You have noticed that when you worship Me in spirit and in truth; you sense My presence. Through your worship, your spirit has moved into the heavenly realm. You always presumed My presence came down from heaven, but in reality your spirit rises up to My throne to meet Me in worship. People often believe that worshipping around My throne will only happen when they go to heaven. Worship is already happening around My throne through the praises of My people on earth. That is why it is written, 'Thy kingdom come thy will be done on earth as it is in heaven.' Pure worship causes your spirit to rise up and become one with Me. I inhabit the praises of My people as their spirit becomes one with Mine."

"Lord, explain how my spirit becomes one with Yours."

"Child, I have spoken these words to you on different occasions: Rise up, rise up and meet the One you call Maker. I was prompting you to become one with Me through worship. Your oneness with Me was first established when you received My Son Jesus Christ as your Savior. The continued unity occurs through worshipping. Why do you think the enemy has tried to destroy pure worship? Satan does not want you to be one with Me. Satan knows the power of unadulterated worship because

I created him to worship Me."

"Lord, define worship as You desire to be worshipped."

"True worship must come from the heart and not be ritualistic. Singing, playing musical instruments, clapping, dancing, bowing, kneeling, lying prostrate, hands held high and twirling joyfully all done with love and adoration to Me is beautiful in My sight, and I receive with great joy."

"Lord, why do certain songs seem to usher me into Your holy presence while others evoke more of a celebration?"

"Pay attention to the words you are singing. Some songs are about man's response to God, and some songs are about what man is going to do for God. These are celebratory songs. Songs of worship that lift your spirit to become one with Me are songs that sing praises directly to Me. For example when you sing 'Glory in the highest to You', or 'Alleluia' or 'Lord, You are Holy.' These words are sung directly to Me, and I inhabit the praises of My people."

The Lord also revealed something else about our worship, and this should cause people really to ponder about praising the Lord. I was in a church setting, and I sensed from the Holy Spirit that I needed to get on my knees in holy reverence as I worshipped. As soon as I knelt, I was lifted into the holy presence of the Lord, and my body began to tremble, and tears streamed down my face. I was worshipping the Lord with every fiber of my being. Then I heard the Holy Spirit tell me to look around. In the Spirit I could see bright beams of light shooting up from individual people in the congregation as they worshipped. The Holy Spirit said that the beams of light represented worship that was rising to the throne of God. Not everyone had a beam of light rising from their head. The

Lord revealed to me that those who did not have a beam of light were people with sin issues in their lives who needed repentance. Their worship was not lifted up to God. The Scripture that came to my mind was this. "Who may ascend into the hill of the LORD? Or who may stand in His holy place? He who has clean hands and a pure heart" (Psalm 24:3-4).

Through pure worship, our spirit can become one with God, but there is another great mystery the Holy Spirit unfolded to me about how we were one with Jesus even before creation. The church has not fully grasped this great mystery. Truly, only the Spirit of God can reveal how we are in Christ and how we are united with Him as one. There is great spiritual power in this teaching because it will enable the church to grasp the fullness of the cross and walk in the power of the completed work of Jesus Christ. We are part of Jesus' body, flesh and bones, and this revelation will transform the lives of God's people. "For we are members of His body, of His flesh and of His bones. For this reason a man shall leave his father and mother and be joined to his wife, and the two shall become one flesh. This is a great mystery, but I speak concerning Christ and the church (Ephesians 5:30-32)."

Those who are seeking a more intimate relationship with the Lord will be empowered by this great mystery. When a biblical truth is unfolded by the unction of the Holy Spirit, it becomes the power to believe the scripture and by faith embrace it as your own. The truth is no longer just mental knowledge; it becomes heart knowledge whereby the truth becomes the very essence of one's being. How are we one with Jesus? How are we a part of His body, flesh and His bones? The answer is that we were in Christ before creation. We were a part of Him; we were a part of His very essence before the beginning of time. Take a moment and let that truth sink into your spirit.

We proceeded from the breath of Christ when He created mankind beginning with Adam and Eve. We came forth from Him as a result of His word. "Then God said, 'Let Us make man in Our image, according to Our likeness'" (Genesis 1:26). All creation proceeded forth from the spoken Word of God! That means us! Our position was in Christ Jesus before He even created man. That is why we are members of His body, His flesh, and His bones! That is also why when Christ went to the cross, we went to the cross with Him and were baptized into His death. We were in Him before creation and the Lamb was slain before creation. We were also buried with Him through this baptism into death because we were in Christ before creation. We were resurrected with Him because we were in Christ before creation. We become a new creation when we receive Christ as our resurrected Savior, and sin no longer has dominion over us! The devil has deceived the church into believing that sin can still control us. Satan does not want you walking in the fullness of the cross. He does not want you to know you were in Christ when Jesus died on the cross and the power of sin was broken! Paul described this wonderful revelation that our old sinful man has been crucified with Christ.

> "What shall we say then? Shall we continue in
> sin that grace may abound? Certainly not! How
> shall we who died to sin live any longer in it?
> Or do you not know that as many of us as were

baptized into Christ Jesus were baptized into His death? Therefore we were buried with Him through baptism into death, that just as Christ was raised from the dead by the glory of the Father, even so we also should walk in newness of life. For if we have been united together in the likeness of His death, certainly we also shall be in the likeness of His resurrection, knowing this, that our old man was crucified with Him, that the body of sin might be done away with, that we should no longer be slaves of sin. For he who has died has been freed from sin. Now if we died with Christ, we believe that we shall also live with Him, knowing that Christ, having been raised from the dead, dies no more. Death no longer has dominion over Him. For the death that He died, He died to sin once for all; but the life that He lives, He lives to God. Likewise you also, reckon yourselves to be dead indeed to sin, but alive to God in Christ Jesus our Lord" (Romans 6:1-11).

Sin no longer has dominion over us because we were crucified with Christ, and the grip of sin was broken because Christ lives within us! "I have been crucified with Christ; it is no longer I who live, but Christ lives in me; and the life which I now live in the flesh I live by faith in the Son of God, who loved me and gave Himself for me" (Galatians 2:20). Paul said that he was a chief sinner before he had his encounter with Jesus. Paul does not say he remained a chief sinner because he was delivered from sin's power. He said he was a former blasphemer and a persecutor of the Christian sect, of which he was now a part. Formerly, he was an insolent man because he used his position and power as a Pharisee for his purposes.

> "And I thank Christ Jesus our Lord who has enabled me, because He counted me faithful, putting me into the ministry, although I was formerly a blasphemer, a persecutor, and an insolent man; but I obtained mercy because I did it ignorantly in unbelief. And the grace of our Lord was exceedingly abundant, with faith and love which are in Christ Jesus. This is a faithful saying and worthy of all acceptance, that Christ Jesus came into the world to save sinners, of whom I am chief" (1 Timothy 1:12-15).

The power of sin was broken in Paul's life because he understood that when Jesus went to the cross and was crucified, he also went to the cross, and the power of sin was done away with in his life. The only way sin can have power over the believer is complete disobedience to God's commands by openly embracing the sin, or being unaware of this wonderful revelation that sin no longer has dominion over them! The born again believer is free from indwelling sin! We are one with Jesus because we were a part of Him before the beginning of time and because He dwells in the believer.

There is second great mystery that Jesus unfolded for me: ***"My child you need to understand My oneness with My Father. I was in My Father and proceeded out from Him. I*** *was not created, for I am eternal. I and My Father are one. This is a great mystery yet to be unfolded. In order for you to understand what John was viewing in the throne room of heaven, you need to understand My Oneness with My Father. When John viewed the One who sat on the throne, he was viewing Me and My Father as One."*

"After these things I looked, and behold, a door standing open in heaven. And the first voice which I heard was like a trumpet speaking with me, saying, 'Come up here, and I will show you things which must take place after this.' Immediately I was in the Spirit; and behold, a throne set in heaven, and One sat on the throne" (Revelation 4:1-2).

"When John wept because no one was worthy to open the scroll, I proceeded out from My Father and stood to take the scroll out of His right hand."

"And I looked, and behold, in the midst of the throne and of the four living creatures, and in the midst of the elders, stood a Lamb as though it had been slain, having seven horns and seven eyes, which are the seven Spirits of God sent out into all the earth. Then He came and took the scroll out of the right hand of Him who sat on the throne" (Revelation 5:6-7).

The oneness I have with My Father is like the oneness I have with My true church. The church existed in Me before the beginning of time. I have existed in the Father eternally, and that is how I am one with My Father. There is only one God."

The oneness of God was identified in scripture through His name so that it would be revered for ages to come. "Moreover God said to Moses, "Thus you shall say to the children of Israel: 'The LORD God of your fathers, the God of Abraham, the God of Isaac, and the God of Jacob, has sent me to you. This is My name forever, and this is My memorial to all generations.'" (Exodus 3:15). The problem that arises is the English translation of God's name has been translated as LORD God and this is not His real name.

Most of the New Testament was written in Aramaic, translated to Greek, and then translated to English. When the original Aramaic text was translated to Greek, they replaced the original names of God with the generic terms God, Lord, or LORD God. It is important we know the God of the universe's real name because it reveals His true identity. Throughout all of scripture names were important because they identified the character and nature of the individual. Names are still important in God's kingdom, especially His name. God's true named revealed in scripture is an everlasting name that will be a memorial to all generations. If His name is to be a memorial to all generations, then it is important that we have His name correct. The scripture in Exodus should read: "Moreover Elohim said to Moses, 'Thus you shall say to the children of Israel: The YHWH of your fathers, the Elohim of Abraham, the Elohim of Isaac, and the Elohim of Jacob, has sent me to you. This is My name forever, and this is My memorial to all generations.'" (Exodus 3:15 AENT).

The name that is to be a memorial for all generations is YHWH (pronounced Yah Weh). The other name that was translated incorrectly in scripture is Jesus. Jesus is not the name of the Son of YHWH. His Son's name is Y'shua (pronounced Ye shu a). This is important because His Aramaic name in scripture identifies His purpose for mankind. It also identifies that He proceeded out from the Father and they are one, but separate. With the English translations of both names, you cannot see the plurality in their oneness which displays their unity but diversity. Y'shua means YHWH saves. YHWH is the true authority and true name of God. Y'shua proceeded from YHWH and is also YHWH .

The Holy Spirit is the Spirit of YHWH! Thus we have the plurality of God as one God. The Jews had difficulty reconciling that Y'shua was God, because in their recitation of the Shema, there is only one God. "Hear, O Israel: The LORD our God, the LORD is one!" (Deuteronomy 6:4). They have a difficult time recognizing that one God can have a plurality but still be one God as the scripture states. The names YHWH and Y'shua explain their relationship because His name is an everlasting name to all generations! Y'shua desperately wanted them to understand the great mystery that He and YHWH were one. "Jesus said to them, "If God were your Father, you would love Me, for I proceeded forth and came from God; nor have I come of Myself, but He sent Me" (John 8:42).

When Jesus prayed for His disciples and for the future of the church, He unfolded the truth about His oneness with His Father in heaven. "I do not pray for these alone, but also for those who will believe in Me through their word; that they all may be one, as You, Father, are in Me, and I in You; that they also may be one in Us, that the world may believe that You sent Me" (John 17: 20-21). The oneness of YHWH and Y'shua gives us a better understanding of the Throne Room in heaven.

There is another activity that will take place in the Throne Room of God that will be an exciting event. This will be a formal affair in heaven accompanied with great joy and celebration. Everyone will be dressed in their robe of righteousness and their garment of salvation. This event will be like a grand wedding with Jesus as the Groom. There will be a great procession of the saints before Jesus Christ. Each person will present their crown to Jesus Christ to honor Him as King. It will be a magnificent day in heaven! The crowns we present to Jesus are a symbol of our submission to the Lord Most High. When a king or high priest was chosen by God, oil was poured on their head, and the Holy Spirit filled them.

The crown upon the king's head represented his submission to God and reminded the people that they were submitting to God's chosen vessel through the king or the high priest. The crowns we will wear in heaven also signify that we are priests and kings of the Lord Most High God. "To Him who loved us and washed us from our sins in His own blood, and has made us kings and priests to His God and Father, to Him be glory and dominion forever and ever. Amen" (Revelation 1:5-6).

The Lord revealed to me that everyone will have a unique crown designed especially for them. He described my crown to me: *"Your crown will be covered in diamonds and rubies. It is a delicate tiara, for you are a delicate woman. It is a beautiful crown, and you will gladly give it back to Me."*

The Lord Jesus also permitted me to view His crown in a vision. I saw Jesus in His Royal robe. The robe was a unique color of deep blue, and it flowed to the floor with an extraordinarily long train. This was the same robe I saw Him wearing in another vision when I saw him on His white horse in the sky with the saints. I saw Him standing there in regal beauty, and my eyes were drawn to the crown that was upon His head. It was a high crown that sat on His head wavy, dark brown hair. It was a pure, vibrant gold with seven pointed tips around the circumference that defined its shape as a royal crown fit for a king. The seven-pointed crown on Jesus' head represents completion and the number of the Spirits of God. The circular shape depicts that He is the Alpha and the Omega without beginning and without end.

~ CHAPTER SIXTEEN ~

The Banquet Room

There are many rooms in heaven, and the Lord showed me a very special one called the Banquet Room. I saw an exquisitely beautiful long table made of highly polished wood. The various light and dark pigment of the wood reminded me of the olive wood I have seen in Israel. At each place setting were stunning gold goblets that were intricately carved and studded with precious gemstones. These goblets lined the table in the Banquet Room and were ready for a big event. The top rims of the goblets were smooth polished gold, and directly below was a band of elaborately carved Aramaic letters that encircled the goblets.

A large ruby was recessed in the center of each goblet, and the Spirit revealed to me that it represented the tribe of Judah. The other eleven gemstones surrounding the ruby were smaller. They represented the other tribes of Israel. The stones on the goblets were the ruby in the center, and then a topaz, emerald, turquoise, sapphire, diamond, jacinth, agate, amethyst, beryl, onyx, and jasper. The stem of the goblets was marvelously carved. There were pomegranates all around the base of the stem, and then further up the stem were lilies. On the narrower part of the goblets' stem was the trunk of a palm tree whose branches flowed into the base of the goblets.

These gold goblets were suburb in craftsmanship, and I pondered why I was shown the intricate details of these beautiful chalices. Pomegranates, palms, and flowers were also used in the décor of Solomon's Temple. "Then he carved all the walls of the temple all around, both the inner and outer sanctuaries, with carved figures of cherubim, palm trees, and open flowers. The capitals on the two pillars also had pomegranates above, by the convex surface which was next to the network; and there were two hundred such pomegranates in rows on each of the capitals all around" (1 Kings 6:29 and 7:20). The Holy Spirit had shown me the details of these goblets for a reason. The palm tree is a symbol of victory, and when Jesus entered Jerusalem, the people spread palm branches before Him as a sign that He was their victorious King. The pomegranate is the symbol of fruitfulness and joy that we have as God's children. The lily is the symbol of beauty and splendor, and Jesus said that even Solomon in all his glory was not arrayed like one of the lilies. The symbols that God used in Solomon's temple are also utilized in the chalices in the Banquet Room in heaven because they represent the fulfillment of the New Covenant. Temple sacrifice fulfilled the requirements under the Old Covenant, and Jesus' sacrificial death fulfilled the New Covenant. On the night Jesus was betrayed, He celebrated the Passover meal with His disciples.

> "And as they were eating, Jesus took bread, blessed and broke it, and gave it to the disciples and said, 'Take, eat; this is My body.' Then He

took the cup, and gave thanks, and gave it to them, saying, 'Drink from it, all of you. For this is My blood of the new covenant, which is shed for many for the remission of sins. But I say to you, I will not drink of this fruit of the vine from now on until that day when I drink it new with you in My Father's kingdom'" (Matthew 26:26-29).

Jesus told His disciples that He would not drink wine with them again until He was in heaven with His Father. The Banquet Room is the place in heaven that this will occur with His disciples. It will also be the place where there will be a great feast held for all who are in heaven.

"Let us be glad and rejoice and give Him glory, for the marriage of the Lamb has come, and His wife has made herself ready. And to her it was granted to be arrayed in fine linen, clean and bright, for the fine linen is the righteous acts of the saints. Then he said to me, 'Write: Blessed are those who are called to the marriage supper of the Lamb!' And he said to me, 'These are the true sayings of God'" (Revelation 19:7-9).

This will be an awesome banquet in heaven, and I was given the honor of viewing the banquet table set with these precious goblets prepared for this great event.

Jesus told a very important parable that was related to this Banquet Room while He was dining at the house of one of the Pharisees on the Sabbath. While Jesus taught the religious leaders, they were stunned into silence as they pondered His teachings and the depth of His knowledge. In this parable Jesus explained that a notable man prepared a great feast and invited his guests. Each of the distinguished guests had an excuse why they could not attend this banquet. A vast amount of food had been already prepared, so he told his servant to go into the streets and bring the poor, the lame, and the blind to his magnificent banquet.

So the servant obeyed and brought these people to this great feast, but there was still room at the table. "Then the master said to the servant, 'Go out into the highways and hedges, and compel them to come in, that my house may be filled'" (Luke 14:23). Through this parable Jesus was preparing the Pharisees for this great heavenly feast in the Banquet Room, but they were refusing His invitation because they did not believe He was sent from God. Their unbelief had disqualified them from partaking of this heavenly banquet. There is a splendid feast waiting for God's children in the Banquet Room in heaven, but there is still room at the table. The Master is compelling His children on earth to go out to the highways and hedges, which are the neighborhoods and cities, and invite people to join this great feast. The only way to secure a place at this beautiful table in the Banquet Room is to know Jesus Christ as Savior. The only way people can know is to hear the good news. The only way they can hear the good news is if someone tells them.

> "How then shall they call on Him in whom they
> have not believed? And how shall they believe
> in Him of whom they have not heard? And how

shall they hear without a preacher? And how shall they preach unless they are sent? As it is written: How beautiful are the feet of those who preach the gospel of peace, Who bring glad tidings of good things!" (Romans 10:14-15).

We have been commissioned by the Lord to invite people to the marriage supper of the Lamb because the King will not begin His banquet with empty seats! The banquet table is ready! I saw it in the Banquet Room, and it is spectacular!

CHAPTER SEVENTEEN

Who's in Heaven

The Old Testament saints are in heaven, along with every person throughout the ages who have repented and received the forgiveness of their sin through Jesus Christ. Without repentance from sin, there is no salvation through Jesus, nor is there eternal life in heaven. It is important to acknowledge that you have sinned and crucial that you turn from your sin. There are false teachings being circulated that a person can repent of their sin after death, and that is a lie from the pit of hell. "Truly, these times of ignorance God overlooked, but now commands all men everywhere to repent, because He has appointed a day on which He will judge the world in righteousness by the Man whom He has ordained. He has given assurance of this to all by raising Him from the dead" (Acts 17:30-31).

It is not enough to know *about* Jesus; even the demons believe in Jesus, and they do not have a place in heaven. What is the difference between believing in Jesus and being truly born again by the Spirit of God? The difference lies within your heart. You become conscious of your sin and admit that you have committed offensive acts that deserve to be punished in hell. You also come to the realization that Jesus took the penalty for your sin by being crucified on the cross, and that He has provided a way to circumvent your punishment. You confess with your mouth that Jesus Christ is God; He rose from the dead, and has the power to give you eternal life because He shed His blood for your transgressions. With sincerity in your heart, you humbly ask Jesus to forgive you and promise to love and obey Him as your Lord and Master. Now you have more than just a mental ascent of Jesus! Your spirit is born again, and you are renewed by the power of the Holy Spirit. You are a new creation in Christ! It is a great spiritual mystery how our spirits are born again, but it must happen to become a child of God.

When you are born again, there are outward changes that reflect the inward transformation. Simply saying a prayer of salvation does not assure you a place in heaven if there is not true repentance and there are no outward changes in your life. Refusing to obey God's commands is a sure sign that you are not born again, and you do not have a place in heaven. Jesus made this statement about those who claim to belong to Him; who claim to be Christians without having been transformed by the Holy Spirit.

> "Not everyone who says to Me, 'Lord, Lord,'
> shall enter the kingdom of heaven, but he who
> does the will of My Father in heaven. Many will
> say to Me in that day, 'Lord, Lord, have we not
> prophesied in Your name, cast out demons in
> Your name, and done many wonders in Your
> name?' And then I will declare to them, 'I never

knew you; depart from Me, you who practice lawlessness!'" (Matthew 7:21-23).

Practicing lawlessness means refusing to obey the laws of God defined by the Word of God. The Ten Commandments are just as valid today as they were three thousand years ago because Jesus did not come to abolish the law; He came to fulfill the law in every point. The Father in heaven wants everyone to repent and all to come to the saving knowledge of Jesus Christ so that none will perish in hell. Unfortunately, many will refuse this narrow way and continue in their sin and unbelief until death, and they will suffer the torments of hell for all eternity. "Enter by the narrow gate; for wide is the gate and broad is the way that leads to destruction, and there are many who go in by it. Because narrow is the gate and difficult is the way which leads to life, and there are few who find it" (Matthew 7:13-14). Heaven is a prepared paradise for all those who have repented of their sin, embraced Jesus' forgiveness, have been born again by the Spirit, and love God by obeying His commands.

Babies and children are also in heaven, and the Lord expounded upon this beautiful truth which gives mothers hope that have lost a child. If you are a mother who has lost a child through death, you can be assured they are in heaven, and you will be reunited with them provided you have committed *your* life to Christ. The Lord said these words to me: ***"Babies that are stillborn, die in the womb, or are aborted are escorted to heaven by one of My angels. This angel will stay with the baby and train up the child in the heavens. There is a special place in heaven for these little ones that never had a chance to live on earth. I love these children, and they*** *fill My heart with joy. They are in My presence, and I am their salvation. There are not years to mark their growth because there is no time in heaven; nonetheless, the child will still go through the developmental stages. My angels teach them. They play and interact with one another."*

"Let the little children come to Me, and do not forbid them; for of such is the kingdom of God. Assuredly, I say to you, whoever does not receive the kingdom of God as a little child will by no means enter it. And He took them up in His arms, laid His hands on them, and blessed them" (Mark 10:14-16). Imagine this scene in heaven. Jesus saunters across a beautiful plush green meadow, and when the children spot Him from a distance, they run towards Him gleefully squealing with delight. Jesus sits down on the grass, and all the children sit eagerly waiting for story time. Some of the children try to push their way to the front to get closer to Jesus, and their angel positions these little ones in their appropriate seat. They are wearing little white gowns and their shining faces excitedly wait to hear Jesus. When Jesus begins to speak, their eyes and attention is riveted on Him. Jesus is indeed their salvation. He rescued them from death's grip, and they get to experience their childhood in heaven! How awesome!

I asked the Lord if there was an age of accountability if an older child dies. So often we hear that term bantered around, and I pondered if it were biblical. The Lord spoke these words to me: *"The age of Bar Mitzvah is the age I require a child to be accountable for their relationship with Me. Upon the completion of twelve years of life; I require a child to follow My commands. My Word instructs parents to train up a child in the ways of God, so he will not depart from*

Me. It is the responsibility of a parent to train a child in My ways, and I will hold parents liable. The child becomes accountable after the twelve years of training."

Bar Mitzvah literally means "son of commandment." A Jewish boy automatically becomes Bar Mitzvah upon reaching the age of thirteen years, and no ceremony is needed to confer these rights and obligations. A century ago there was no Bar Mitzvah celebration needed to become accountable to God's commands, and the modern celebration of Bar Mitzvah is not recorded in the Talmud. Scriptures are silent about Jesus' childhood until His encounter with the religious teachers at the Temple in Jerusalem. For three days Jesus questioned and listened to the religious leaders, and they were amazed at His understanding and knowledge of the Torah. It is significant that Luke mentioned Jesus was twelve years old during this Passover when He was in the Temple. Jesus knew He would be Bar Mitzvah at age thirteen, and He was acutely aware He would be accountable to follow the commands of His Father just like every other child His age. He spent those three days with the religious leaders to make sure His knowledge of the scripture was sound, and even they were amazed at His knowledge.

Although today, only the Jews celebrate Bar Mitzvah for their children to acknowledge their accountability to follow God's commands; all children are accountable to follow God's commands at age thirteen. Abraham was ninety-nine years old and Ishmael was thirteen years old when God established circumcision as the outward sign of His covenant. It is very noteworthy that Ishmael was circumcised at thirteen because this established his accountability to God, even though he was not the son of promise.

Throughout scripture, the accountability to follow God's commands was established not just for the nation of Israel because Ishmael was circumcised along with Abraham. After Isaac was born, Ishmael mocked Isaac; and as a result, he and his mother were expelled from Abraham's household. Ishmael was held accountable for his distain of God's chosen son, who would be the descendant of the twelve tribes of Israel. Although Ishmael became the father of twelve gentile nations, it did not change their responsibility and liability to follow God's commands. In other words, Bar Mitzvah was for every child over the age of twelve whether they were Jew or gentile. That same principle still holds true today, and every child over the age of twelve will be held accountable for their relationship with God, and this will determine their eternal destination at death. Children over the age of twelve that die without Christ as their Savior will answer for their decision.

~ CHAPTER EIGHTEEN ~

Angels and Messengers

Angels and messengers of the Lord play an integral part in both the heavenly and earthly realms. They are created beings with a free will that serve God in many capacities. Scriptures indicate they are innumerable, have supernatural power, can travel quickly from heaven to earth, can appear in the form of a man, deliver messages of God, protect people and nations, and release God's judgments. There is a fascination with angels and the supernatural because our spirits long to connect with anything associated with God. God is Spirit, and He is supernatural. We desire to know more about Him through the spiritual realm that surrounds Him. The angels surround God's throne constantly, and getting a glimpse of the workings of the heavenly realm satisfies an innate desire to connect with our Maker.

The Seraphim are angels that were created to declare the holiness of God, and they never leave the presence of God. These seraphim worship and give glory and thanks to Him who sits on the throne. "Above it stood seraphim; each one had six wings: with two he covered his face, with two he covered his feet, and with two he flew. And one cried to another and said:

'Holy, holy, holy *is* the LORD of hosts; The whole earth *is* full of His glory!'" (Isaiah 6:1-3). These angels were uniquely created to be in the presence of God continually. They are the only six winged angels mentioned in scripture. One set of wings covered their face because no one can behold the majesty of God the Father and remain alive except Jesus. The other set of wings covered their feet because they were standing in a sacred realm of complete holiness. When the Lord appeared to Moses and Joshua, they were instructed to remove their sandals because they were standing on holy ground. The ground was made holy by the manifest presence of God. These seraphim are not permitted to wear sandals because they are on holy ground, so they cover their feet with the second set of wings. They fly with the third set of wings.

The cherubim were four winged angels with two wings that went straight up and touched the wings of the other cherub as they surrounded the throne of God. There were only four cherubim because there are four directions; north, south, east, and west. When their wings touch each other, they form a complete circle without beginning or end which speaks of God's eternality. Their other two wings cover their body and conceal the form of a man's hands. Their legs were straight with their feet appearing like bronze colored calves feet. They had four different faces on one head which would be a peculiar sight to behold. The face of a man, the face of an ox, the face of an eagle, and the face of a lion comprised the head of the cherubim.

The Lord gave me this explanation about the cherubim: *"All of My creation is embodied in these angels. When the cherubim worship Me, all of creation is worshipping Me.*

The face of the man and the hands of the man represent the human race. The face of the oxen and the feet of the calf represent the animals which were also used to sacrifice in the Temple. The face of the eagle represents the birds of the air. The face of the lion represents the beasts of the field. I also created the cherubim to have four faces to be a representation of My Son. He would come in the form of a man, be sacrificed as the Lamb of God so the sacrifice of calves was no longer needed. He would rise from the dead just as the eagle rises up, and He is the Lion of the tribe of Judah. There are a multitude of angels and each one has a purpose. The cherubim and the seraphim have four faces, but other angels only have one face. Lucifer was a cherub before he rebelled against Me, but I did not permit him or the other rebellious angels to retain My original design. The fallen angels are now demons and unclean spirits. They are vile looking, putrid smelling, and their voices have become corrupt. They can no longer sing, and their voices are guttural, raspy and screechy."

Ezekiel observed another phenomenon about these angelic beings called cherubim that was very unusual. There were wheels within wheels that contained the spirit of these living creatures. Everywhere the cherubim went; these wheels that contained their spirit went simultaneously with them

> "As for the likeness of the living creatures, their appearance was like burning coals of fire, like the appearance of torches going back and forth among the living creatures. The fire was bright, and out of the fire went lightning.

And the living creatures ran back and forth, in appearance like a flash of lightning. Now as I looked at the living creatures, behold, a wheel was on the earth beside each living creature with its four faces. The appearance of the wheels and their workings was like the color of beryl, and all four had the same likeness. The appearance of their workings was, as it were, a wheel in the middle of a wheel. When they moved, they went toward any one of four directions; they did not turn aside when they went. As for their rims, they were so high they were awesome; and their rims were full of eyes, all around the four of them. When the living creatures went, the wheels went beside them; and when the living creatures were lifted up from the earth, the wheels were lifted up. Wherever the spirit wanted to go, they went, because there the spirit went; and the wheels were lifted together with them, for the spirit of the living creatures was in the wheels" (Ezekiel 1:13-20).

Ezekiel described the spirit of the cherubim as a wheel and another separate wheel turning inside. Whenever the wheel moved, then the cherubim moved because the spirit of the cherubim was in the wheel. The outer rim of the wheel was covered in eyes, and the cherubim and the wheels move with God on His throne. Wherever the presence of God is, the cherubim are also with Him. The eyes of the wheels of the cherubim search the earth on behalf of God. "For the eyes of the LORD run to and fro throughout the whole earth, to show Himself strong on behalf of those whose heart is loyal to Him" (2 Chronicles 16:9). This is a comforting and reassuring truth to know that God searches for those who are loyal to Him so He can manifest His power in their lives. These cherubim escort God when He is traveling to the earthly realm, and Ezekiel saw them in a vision accompanying God.

God gave Moses His instruction to build the Ark of the Covenant, and the plans included two cherubim to be molded out of gold for the cover of the ark. "And you shall make two cherubim of gold; of hammered work you shall make them at the two ends of the mercy seat. And there I will meet with you, and I will speak with you from above the mercy seat, from between the two cherubim which are on the ark of the Testimony, about everything which I will give you in commandment to the children of Israel" (Exodus 25:18 and 22).

The presence of God rested between these gold cherubim on the cover of the ark and was a type to show that God moves in the earthly realm with His cherubim. These cherubim move quickly about the earth collecting information and viewing the earth; they act like a satellite that provides important information. But these cherubim are a much faster heavenly information highway. The spirit of the cherubim was separate from its body which was a detail that was revealed to Ezekiel for a reason.

God created the angels as well as creating man, but the angels were not created in the likeness of God. Man is a tri-part being of body, soul and spirit. The spirit of man is not a separate entity of man, like the spirit of the cherubim. Since we are created in the image of God; then it goes without saying that God is also a tri- part being of body, soul and spirit. God is not some mystical spirit that floats in heaven. He has a body; He has a soul comprised of a mind, will and emotions; and He has a Spirit. The angels do not know what it is like to be formed in the image of God, and they desire to have knowledge about man's salvation through God's Son. "Of this salvation ...which now have been reported to you through those who have preached the gospel to you by the Holy Spirit sent from heaven—things which angels desire to look into" (1 Peter 1:12). It is amazing that even the cherubim, who are in the constant presence of God; desire to experience what has been given to man. The angels desire to know what it is like to have the God of the universe dwelling in them!

Every detail in scripture is written for a reason, and the Lord opened up His treasures of revelation regarding the movement of these angelic beings that accompany Him. These cherubim traveled in a distinct manner because they never turned aside; they only moved toward any of the four directions. The cherubim only moved forward, backward, to the left and to the right which means they can only move north, south, east and west. This motion forms a cross! This reveals how intricately God takes into account all the details of His creation.

Angels are not constricted by time or space. They can use their wings to move, or they can teleport from one place to another very quickly. They are not flesh and blood, so they can move through space quickly and travel through solid objects if necessary. They can also take on different forms and can take on the form of a man without us being aware that it is an angel. "Do not forget to entertain strangers, for by so doing some have unwittingly entertained angels" (Hebrews 13:2).

Angels are very large and very powerful, and they carefully carry out God's instructions. "Bless the LORD, you His angels, Who excel in strength, who do His word, Heeding the voice of His word. Bless the LORD, all you His hosts, You ministers of His, who do His pleasure" (Psalm 103:20-21). One of the reasons angels are hidden from our view as they carry out God's instructions is because they would cause fear, intimidation, and their overwhelming presence would be distracting. The thundering of their voice would be terrifying. "Then the Spirit lifted me up, and I heard behind me a great thunderous voice: 'Blessed is the glory of the LORD from His place!' I also heard the noise of the wings of the living creatures that touched one another, and the noise of the wheels beside them, and a great thunderous noise" (Ezekiel 3:12-14).

Archangels are another class of angels mentioned, and only one is named as an archangel in scripture. "Yet Michael the archangel, in contending with the devil, when he disputed about the body of Moses, dared not bring against him a reviling accusation, but said, 'The Lord rebuke you!'" (Jude 9). The archangels are assigned earthly, as well as heavenly duties. Angels are not omnipresent, so they must travel from one area to another. An angel was dispatched by God to bring Daniel an explanation of future events, but this angel was detained by the prince of Persia who was the demonic principality over that region. For twenty-one days this angel was detained until Michael came to the rescue.

"But the prince of the kingdom of Persia

withstood me twenty-one days; and behold, Michael, one of the chief princes, came to help me, for I had been left alone there with the kings of Persia. And now I must return to fight with the prince of Persia; and when I have gone forth, indeed the prince of Greece will come. But I will tell you what is noted in the Scripture of Truth. (No one upholds me against these, except Michael your prince" (Daniel 10:13, 20-21).

Archangels have more power and strength than other angels, and they are assigned to certain regions. Michael is the chief prince over Israel. He is a warrior angel that frequently does battle on behalf of Israel, and he has an army of angels that accompany him. Just as Israel is surrounded by earthly enemies that want to destroy her people, there are unseen enemies that also want to destroy the Jewish nation. There is a spiritual battle being waged for control of the land, and this battle is manifested in the natural realm when neighboring countries demand the land of Israel. Syria demands the Golan Heights, and the Palestinians demand Jerusalem be split for their state. Gaza, which was Israeli land given to the Palestinians, now fire missiles into Israel. We need to pray for the peace of Jerusalem, for those prayers empower Michael and his army against the unseen forces of the enemy. When the spiritual battle is won in the heavens, then the earthly victory follows.

Messenger angels bring God's message, make announcements, and issue instruction and warnings. Gabriel brought God's message to Zechariah that Elizabeth would have a son named John and brought a message to Mary that she would conceive a son by the power of the Holy Spirit, and His name would be Jesus. Gabriel was sent to Daniel to interpret the vision of future events and gave him the skill to understand. A messenger angel was sent to Philip to tell him to go to Gaza, and an angel was sent to Peter to rescue him from prison. An angel appeared to Cornelius to instruct him to send for Peter in Joppa. Angels also declare warnings to the people. An angel warned Joseph to go to Egypt to protect Jesus from being killed by Herod. During the seven-year tribulation, angels will announce warnings to people on the earth, but unfortunately, most will not heed their warnings.

Ministering angels are sent by God to assist, strengthen, and protect people. God the Father sent ministering angels to Jesus after He was tempted by Satan in the wilderness. After forty days of fasting and prayer, the enemy came when Jesus physical body was at its weakest, but His spirit was at its strongest and in tune with His Father. "Then Jesus said to him, 'Away with you, Satan! For it is written, *You shall worship the LORD your God, and Him only you shall serve.*' Then the devil left Him, and behold, angels came and ministered to Him" (Matthew 4:10-11).

God sent an angel to shut the mouths of the lions and protect Daniel when Nebuchadnezzar threw him in the lion's den. Angels are also sent to minister to the sons and daughters of God. "But to which of the angels has He ever said: 'Sit at My right hand, Till I make Your enemies Your footstool? Are they not all ministering spirits sent forth to minister for those who will inherit salvation?'" (Hebrews 1:13-14). Every child of God has one or more angels assigned to him for protection and strength. There are many times when these angels keep us from harm, and we are not aware of their intervention.

These ministering angels know the perfect will of God, and they know when to intervene in our lives and when not to. I have angels protecting me everywhere I go. The Holy Spirit has told me that I have twelve angels assigned to me because that is His number of divine government. They form a circle around me facing outward, and a few people have told me they have witnessed these angels surrounding me.

When I was in a remote village in Malawi in southern Africa, God's protection was with me through my ministering angels. I was preaching and teaching in a remote village where there is no electricity or running water. That evening, I was in the home of a pastor, placing a straw mat on the dirt floor preparing my room to sleep. My flashlight shone on the wall to reveal a very large unfamiliar insect. I called for help, while my eyes remained riveted on this strange creature. When help arrived, he told me it was a scorpion, and its bite was more venomous than a deadly snake. If I were bitten, I would have died.

This man of God also perceived that this scorpion was sent by the power of witchcraft because the area we were ministering was inundated with sorcery. The enemy had sent this deadly scorpion to stop the work of the Lord because there was a great harvest of souls being birthed into the kingdom of God. God's angels always surround me when I travel into the remote villages of the nations, and no weapon formed against me shall prosper until God says my time on earth is finished. The Lord also revealed to me there is another ministering angel that records my writings for my books and presents them to God. As I write material for my books, I ask the Lord to guide me, and I pray fervently that I only write what He desires to be presented. I go over my manuscript line by line and ask the Lord to add or revise anything that I have written. The Lord has carte blanche with my books because they truly are His work; I am just His handmaiden whom He has chosen to reveal such great treasures.

Escorting angels carry God's children to heaven when they breathe their last breath on earth. These escorting angels will also accompany those who are caught up in the sky during the rapture. "Then they will see the Son of Man coming in the clouds with great power and glory. And then He will send His angels, and gather together His elect from the four winds, from the farthest part of earth to the farthest part of heaven" (Mark 13:26-27). Along with escorting angels, there are also death angels as a part of God's hierarchy of angels. Death angels bring God's judgment upon people because of their unbelief and their sin.

> "So the four angels, who had been prepared for the hour and day and month and year, were released to kill a third of mankind. But the rest of mankind, who were not killed by these plagues, did not repent of the works of their hands, that they should not worship demons, and idols of gold, silver, brass, stone, and wood, which can neither see nor hear nor walk. And they did not repent of their murders or their sorceries or their sexual immorality or their thefts" (Revelation 9:15, 20).

There are seven angels that will release God's judgment in the final plagues upon the earth and mankind. The fifth angel will release demonic locusts from the Bottomless Pit to torture man because of his unbelief and rebellious heart towards God, but all those with God's seal on their forehead cannot be bitten by these hideous demons. The Lord spoke these words to me regarding His angels that release His judgment: ***"There are angels that bring My hand of judgment to the people on the earth, but most people refuse to make the connection of sin with My judgment. The earthquake and tsunami that devastated Japan was released by My angel as judgment for the nation's sins. I am about to release another angel in a similar fashion as My judgment on the United States of America for the nation's sin. My angel will be released for a major earthquake that will produce a catastrophic tsunami which will devastate parts of the west coast of America. Sin abounds in the United States, and My judgment is coming. The matter is settled; this calamity will surely happen. Even though I have spoken that this earthquake will happen, many will still not believe it is My judgment, and they will continue in sin."***

There are angels that are assigned to churches that perform various duties. There was an angel assigned to each of the seven churches in the book of Revelation, and there are angels assigned to churches today. They guard the doors, surround the pastor, record the tithes and offering, observe the worship, and record the prayers of the people. These angels are a part of every gathering done in the Name of Jesus. Every time there is a Sunday service, a prayer meeting in a home, a small cell group studying the Word of God or an individual worshipping the Lord, there is an angel is present. Although we are not to focus on the angels, they are very much a part of the spiritual realm that God created for His purposes. We should rejoice in God's provisions, protection, and strength through these heavenly angels that minister to His children who will inherit salvation.

Not only are there angels in heaven and on the earth, but there was an Angel of the Lord that was a special Messenger. This special Messenger was an appearance of Jesus Christ before He took on the form of a man. Jesus appeared several times on earth to men to deliver God's message before He lived on earth. One of the key clues that these appearances were a theophany of Jesus and not an ordinary angel was that this Angel of the Lord permitted people to worship Him. When the Apostle John saw a certain angel, he tried to bow down and worship it, but the angel rebuked him. "And I fell at his feet to worship him. But he said to me, 'See that you do not do that! I am your fellow servant, and of your brethren who have the testimony of Jesus. Worship God! For the testimony of Jesus is the spirit of prophecy'" (Revelation 19:10). Angels will not receive worship because only God is worthy of our worship and praise. It is idolatry to worship and pray to angels, saints, Mary, statues, icons or any other man made form.

There was a divine purpose for each of the visitations of Jesus Christ because it foreshadowed His incarnation in matters of grace and judgment. Today many people focus on God's grace without ever considering God's judgment because their perception of Jesus is skewed. "Jesus Christ is the same yesterday, today, and forever" (Hebrews 13:8). Each of these theophanies of Christ unfolds a more complete picture of the

Son of God and God's plan for humanity. The first appearances of the pre-incarnate Christ were to establish God's promise of the land to Israel; for this was the place on earth He chose to be born, to live, and to die for all humanity.

Jesus appeared to Abraham when he first entered into the land of Canaan, and when he was ninety-nine years old. Each appearance was to clarify God's promises to Abraham so that God's plan for redemption would be set in motion through the nation of Israel. "Then the LORD appeared to Abram and said, 'To your descendants I will give this land.' And there he built an altar to the LORD, who had appeared to him" (Genesis 12:7). God's promise of this land was an everlasting promise. Although Israel was driven from their land because of their idolatry, God never reneged on His promise. He brought His people back to the land after the Babylonian captivity, after the destruction of the first Temple and after the destruction of the second Temple in Jerusalem. Israel was once again established as a nation in 1948 as a fulfillment to God's covenant with Abraham that the land would be an everlasting possession. "And I will establish My covenant between Me and you and your descendants after you in their generations, for an everlasting covenant, to be God to you and your descendants after you. Also I give to you and your descendants after you the land in which you are a stranger, all the land of Canaan, as an everlasting possession; and I will be their God" (Genesis 17:7-8).

The Arab nations which are the descendants of Ishmael have a difficult time recognizing that this land belongs to the descendants of Abraham, Isaac, and Jacob. God gave this land to Abraham as an everlasting possession, and any nation that tries to rip it out of Israel's possession will have to answer to God. In the past, God has judged every nation that has taken possession of Israel's land. The Babylonian, Media Persian, Grecian and Roman empires were all judged by God for taking possession of Israel's land and dispersing the people. Using the land of Israel as a bargaining tool for peace will bring God's hand of judgment. Every time the United States government has used its influence to persuade Israel to give up her land for peace, there have been natural disasters in our country within one or two days that have taken the lives of our people. Our government leaders are blinded to this correlation, and they persist on putting pressure on Israel to give up her land to the Palestinians.

Another theophany of Jesus was the king of Salem named Melchizedek. After Abraham had rescued Lot and the people of Sodom from captivity, Melchizedek met Abraham. This was a theophany of Jesus because this king had no beginning and no end, he was an everlasting priest, and Abraham felt compelled to give one tenth of all of possessions.

> "For this Melchizedek, king of Salem, priest
> of the Most High God, who met Abraham
> returning from the slaughter of the kings
> and blessed him, to whom also Abraham
> gave a tenth part of all, first being translated
> 'king of righteousness,' and then also king of
> Salem, meaning 'king of peace,' without father,
> without mother, without genealogy, having
> neither beginning of days nor end of life, but
> made like the Son of God, remains a priest

continually. Now consider how great this man was, to whom even the patriarch Abraham gave a tenth of the spoils. And indeed those who are of the sons of Levi, who receive the priesthood, have a commandment to receive tithes from the people according to the law, that is, from their brethren, though they have come from the loins of Abraham; but he whose genealogy is not derived from them received tithes from Abraham and blessed him who had the promises" (Hebrews 7:1-6).

Abraham gave a tenth of all of his belongings to the Son of God hundreds of years before God established the tithe to the Levites. This theophany of Jesus was the foreshadowing of His coming and set the principle for tithing under the New Covenant. Many people do not tithe because they do not understand that all they possess is a gift from God and that God requires one tenth of all that He has given them. This principle of tithing was established by Christ as way to honor God as Jehovah Jireh; God our provider. There are blessings that come with tithing, but those blessing are not necessarily financial blessings. God chooses how He will bless us for honoring Him with our tithes. Those blessings could be good health, protection from your enemy, spiritual wisdom, inner peace in dire circumstances, the ability to reach more souls with the Gospel; the list is endless in God's kingdom!

A theophany that most people are familiar with is when God appeared to Moses in the burning bush. This appearance of Christ came at time that was crucial for the nation of Israel.

They had been living in Egypt for the past four hundred years under the harsh treatment of the pharaoh. Pharaoh had enslaved them because he feared the massive population of the Hebrews could revolt against him. God heard the cries of His people, and He decided it was time for the Israelites to take possession of the land that He had promised Abraham.

God commissioned Moses to be His deliverer, and it began with the theophany of Jesus in the burning bush. When Jesus appointed Moses at the burning bush to be God's mouthpiece to Pharaoh, it was the precursor of Jesus appointing apostles, prophets, evangelist, pastors and teachers to be God's mouthpieces under the New Covenant. Jesus delegated the duty to Moses to be God's deliverer, just as Jesus entrusts duties and ministry to His children today. Moses tried to use the excuse that he had a speech impediment and was not a good communicator, but God chose him regardless. It is very interesting how God will call a person into ministry that is weak in a certain area so that He can strengthen them, and then all the glory is given to God.

I remember when I was in high school and I had to stand before my peers and give a speech. My legs were shaking, my voice was cracking, and my stomach was upset. After I made it through that ordeal, I vowed I would never again go before an audience and give a speech. Little did I know that God had other plans, and He would call me to be His evangelist, and I would stand before nations and preach the Gospel! God chooses to use our weakness for His glory because He is not as interested in our ability as much as He is interested in our obedience. God is not limited to our talents or our finances when it comes to serving Him. I have found the bigger the exploit for God, the bigger God becomes because our faith rises up and says nothing is impossible with God! God gave Moses a huge exploit to accomplish for Him, and He supplied an entire package of supernatural phenomenon to accompany God's message to Pharaoh. God has given His church an enormous mission to take His Gospel to the ends of the earth, and He has given us an arsenal of spiritual gifts, signs, and wonders! To God be all the glory!

The next theophany of Jesus was identified as an angel or messenger that would go before the Israelites so they could possess the Promised Land.

> "Behold, I send an Angel before you to keep you in the way and to bring you into the place which I have prepared. Beware of Him and obey His voice; do not provoke Him, for He will not pardon your transgressions; for My name is in Him. But if you indeed obey His voice and do all that I speak, then I will be an enemy to your enemies and an adversary to your adversaries. For My Angel will go before you and bring you in to the Amorites and the Hittites and the Perizzites and the Canaanites and the Hivites and the Jebusites; and I will cut them off" (Exodus 23:20-23).

Angels do not have the power or authority to forgive sin, which establishes this Angel as an appearance of Jesus. God the Father sent Jesus to keep the Israelites on His path to ensure they would take possession of the land that was promised to Abraham.

This was such a beautiful picture of God's grace that the Messiah was sent as a Messenger who led the people into the very place where He would be crucified! The Father instructed the people to obey Y'shua's voice because Yahweh's name was in Him. This theophany of Jesus was God's promise to save people from the power of sin and deliver them from the oppression of Satan. Jesus fulfilled this prophetic theophany when He came to the earth as a man, was crucified on the cross as the perfect sinless Lamb of God, and rose from the dead on the third day.

When the Israelites were about to enter into the Promised Land, God instructed Joshua to circumcise all the males because they had not been circumcised along the way. On the plains of Jericho, they celebrated the Passover and feasted on the food of the land, and from that day forward the manna from heaven ceased.

> "And it came to pass, when Joshua was by Jericho, that he lifted his eyes and looked, and behold, a Man stood opposite him with His sword drawn in His hand. And Joshua went to Him and said to Him, 'Are You for us or for our adversaries?' So He said, 'No, but as Commander of the army of the LORD I have now come.' And Joshua fell on his face to the earth and worshiped, and said to Him, 'What does my Lord say to His servant?' Then the Commander of the LORD's army said to Joshua, 'Take your sandal off your foot, for the place where you stand is holy.' And Joshua did so" (Joshua 5:13-15).

This is a theophany of Jesus Christ because Joshua fell on his face and worshipped the Commander of the army. An ordinary angel would not have permitted or received Joshua's worship. God wanted Joshua to know he was standing in the presence of a holy God and to know how important it was to follow His instructions. The Son of God was there to make sure that His Father's plans were being fulfilled, and this assured Joshua how intricately God was involved in the lives of His people. God had instructed the Israelites to go into the land and possess it and drive out all the inhabitants or else their gods would become a snare to them. Israel did not obey the Lord, and many of the tribes of Israel put the Canaanites under tribute and did not completely drive them out.

As a result of their disobedience, another Angel of the Lord appeared to the Israelites to pronounce judgment. This judgment reveals the side of Jesus that people do not want to acknowledge because they only want to see Him as a God of grace. As a result of their disobedience, Jesus would no longer drive out Israel's enemies. They would have to drive them out in their own strength or tolerate their coexistence which would result in worshipping their gods and more of God's judgment.

"Then the Angel of the LORD came up from Gilgal to Bochim, and said: 'I led you up from Egypt and brought you to the land of which I swore to your fathers; and I said, *I will never break My covenant with you. And you shall make no covenant with the inhabitants of this land; you shall tear down their altars. But you have not obeyed My voice. Why have you done this? Therefore I also said, I will not drive them out before you; but they shall be thorns in your side, and their gods shall be a snare to you.'* So it was, when the Angel of the LORD spoke these words to all the children of Israel, that the people lifted up their voices and wept" (Judges 2:1-4).

There is always a price to pay for disobeying God. All throughout the book of Judges there was a cycle of disobedience to God which resulted in His hand of protection being removed. The Israelites would do evil in the sight of God by worshipping the Baals and Asherahs, and then God's anger would be kindled against Israel, and He would permit Israel's enemies to defeat them. When the children of Israel cried out to God because of the bondage, God would deliver them by an appointed leader who became the judge of Israel. As long as the judge lived, Israel would follow God. But as soon as the judge died, Israel would fall right back into idol worship, and God's anger would be hot against Israel.

Once again they would be overtaken by their enemies until they cried out to God who would raise another judge. This cycle of disobedience and deliverance continued throughout Israel's history, which shows God's great patience while disciplining His children for idolatry. It was during one of these cycles that the Midianites were severely punishing Israel to the point they had become impoverished. An Angel of the Lord appeared to Gideon to pronounce that he was going to deliver the Israelites from the oppression of the Midianites.

"Now the Angel of the LORD came and sat under the terebinth tree which was in Ophrah, which belonged to Joash the Abiezrite, while his son Gideon threshed wheat in the winepress, in order to hide it from the Midianites. And the Angel of the LORD appeared to him, and said to him, 'The LORD is with you, you mighty man of valor!' Gideon said to Him, 'O my lord, if the LORD is with us, why then has all this happened to us? And where are all His miracles which our fathers told us about, saying, Did not the LORD bring us up from Egypt? But now the LORD has forsaken us and delivered us into the hands of the Midianites.' Then the LORD turned to him and said, 'Go in this might of yours, and you shall save Israel from the hand of the Midianites. Have I not sent you?'" (Judges 6:11-14).

This cycle of sin and grace during the period of Judges is the foreshadowing of the incarnate Christ. You cannot have grace without the reality of a coming judgment. If there is no judgment of God for sin; then there was no need for grace. Grace is the unmerited gift needed for the forgiveness of sin. If the judgment of God does not exist, then there was no need for the Son of God to be crucified for our sins. Just because we now live in an age of grace does not mean that the God of the universe has laid His judgment aside.

It is true that those who have received Jesus' forgiveness and are born again by the Spirit of God do not have to fear the judgment of God. Nonetheless, Jesus remains a God of judgment for those who are not saved. God still judges the collective sin of nations although most people refuse to see it as God's hand of judgment because it doesn't fit into their preconceived image of God. God uses earthquakes, tsunamis, hurricanes, tornadoes, flooding, famine, wars and political strife as His hand of judgment against nations for their sin.

Conclusion

Deep down within everyone's soul is a measure of knowledgez of God that will be awakened by His Spirit if a person seeks to know the truth. He is the God of Abraham, Isaac and Jacob. He is the Maker of the heavens and earth and all that is below the earth. He is the one true God, the Alpha and the Omega, without beginning and without end, the everlasting eternal great I Am. God will not share His glory with anyone. He will not share His glory with Muhammad (Islam), John Smith Jr. (Mormons), Charles Taze Russell (Jehovah Witness), Mary Baker Eddy (Christian Science), Ron Hubbard (Scientology), Sun Myung Moon (Unification Church), Charles and Myrtle Fillmore (Unity School of Christianity), Wallace D. Fard (Nation of Islam), Siyyid Ali-Muhammad and Mirza Husayn (Baha'i World Faith), A.C. Bhakivedanta Swami Prabhupada (Hare Krishna), Maharishi Mahesh Yogi (Transcendental Meditation), Gautama Siddhartha (Buddhism), Gerald Gardner (Wicca), the many sects of Hinduism, or even the Catholic Pope who has been venerated as infallible.

If you want to know this one true God, then I invite

you simply to ask Him to show you the truth. Ask the God of the universe to make Himself known to you in a way that you will have no doubt that He is God. All religions that have been established and founded by men and women are alternate doors to heaven that the enemy has created to deceive people. These doors lead straight to hell. There is only one door to enter heaven, and that door is Jesus Christ.

Sometimes it is difficult to believe in things that are not tangible to our senses, but it does not make them nonexistent. Faith is a key component in any belief system, but it is extremely important to place your faith in the right person. "Now faith is the substance of things hoped for, the evidence of things not seen" (Hebrews 11:1). The three key words in this scripture are faith, substance, and evidence. Faith means believing in something with an unwavering assurance and conviction. There is a constant profession of that belief and confidence in the truth of God. "Let us hold fast the confession of our faith without wavering, for He who promised is faithful" (Hebrews 10:23). We need to hold fast to our faith in Jesus Christ whereby we have been delivered from the bondage of sin, we have His provisions and blessings, and we have His protection and love. Faith says that we have a faithful God whose promises are true and His Word is truth.

Substance is the support set under something to establish an assurance of a truth. Visualize a pillar supporting a building. The pillar is the substance that holds up and establishes God's covenant, and Jesus is the substance or the pillar in this scripture. He established and holds up the New Covenant by His Word. In scripture, the Word is defined three ways, and each one is the substance of our faith!

1. The Word - Jesus Christ

"In the beginning was the Word, and the Word was with God, and the Word was God" (John 1:1). "For there are three that bear witness in heaven: the Father, the Word, and the Holy Spirit; and these three are one" (1 John 5:7). "He was clothed with a robe dipped in blood, and His name is called The Word of God" (Revelation 19:3).

2. The Word - Written form of the Bible (Logos)

"For the word of God is living and powerful, and sharper than any two-edged sword, piercing even to the division of soul and spirit, and of joints and marrow, and is a discerner of the thoughts and intents of the heart" (Hebrews 4:12).

3. The Word - Spoken from God (Rhema)

"By faith we understand that the worlds were framed by the word of God, so that the things which are seen were not made of things which are visible" (Hebrews 11:3).

"Then Mary said, 'Behold the maidservant of the Lord! Let it be to me according to your word.' And the angel departed from her" (Luke 1:38).

Evidence is the proof or conviction of something. Even though we have never met Jesus face to face, we have an unwavering conviction and proof that He is our Messiah. We have evidence of Him through the Word of God, the Holy Spirit, and the witness in our spirits that He is the Son of God. This evidence backs up the substance, and the substance supports the faith! "Jesus said to him, 'Thomas, because you have seen Me, you have believed. Blessed are those who have not seen and yet have believed'" (John 20:29).

Even though most have never seen heaven or hell, we have evidence of their existence through the Word of God, the Holy Spirit, and the witness in our spirits. We believe with unwavering assurance and conviction that God's plan of salvation will result in eternal life in heaven. We constantly profess that belief to others, and we have confidence in God's word to us. We begin to take the steps toward those plans God has revealed to us by obeying His commands. We understand that Jesus established God's Word, and His word cannot return to Him empty.

> "So shall My word be that goes
> forth from My mouth;
> It shall not return to Me void,
> But it shall accomplish what I please,
> And it shall prosper in the thing
> for which I sent it"
> (Isaiah 55:11).

When Jesus establishes a thing, it is already accomplished because God spoke it! Don't doubt God's promises to you; start walking in obedience to the things God has revealed to you. When God speaks, it will happen! There is no doubt and no double-mindedness! When God speaks into your life about His plans for you, God sees it as already completed. The problem arises when you do not see it the same way as God sees it. Faith is seeing things the way God sees things and calling them already accomplished when they have yet to be fulfilled. The things God speaks are substance! You have the guarantee and the underlying support you need to follow His plan. Even though you cannot see into the future, God knows all things, and He guides you every step of the way. You can have an unwavering conviction that God's plans will be fulfilled even though you have not yet seen them. As you profess God's plans, there is an internal assurance and confidence they will come to pass. As you profess your faith in Jesus Christ, you have a steadfast promise that heaven is your eternal destination. Elijah was a perfect example of the working out of his faith in God.

> "And Elijah the Tishbite, of the inhabitants of Gilead, said to Ahab, 'As the LORD God of Israel lives, before whom I stand, there shall not be dew nor rain these years, except at my word.' Then the word of the LORD came to him, saying, 'Get away from here and turn eastward, and hide by the Brook Cherith, which flows into the Jordan. And it will be that you shall drink from the brook, and I have commanded the ravens to feed you there.' So he went and did according to the word of the LORD, for he went and stayed by the Brook Cherith, which flows into the Jordan. The ravens brought him bread and meat in the morning, and bread and meat in the evening; and he drank from the brook. And it happened after a while that the brook dried up because there had been no rain in the land. Then the word of the LORD came to him, saying, 'Arise, go to Zarephath, which belongs to Sidon, and dwell there. See, I have

commanded a widow there to provide for you.' So he arose and went to Zarephath. And it came to pass after many days that the word of the LORD came to Elijah, in the third year, saying, 'Go, present yourself to Ahab, and I will send rain on the earth.' And Elijah went up to the top of Carmel; then he bowed down on the ground, and put his face between his knees, and said to his servant, 'Go up now, look toward the sea.' So he went up and looked, and said, 'There is nothing.' And seven times he said, 'Go again.' Then it came to pass the seventh time, that he said, 'There is a cloud, as small as a man's hand, rising out of the sea!' So he said, 'Go up, say to Ahab, *Prepare your chariot, and go down before the rain stops you.*' Now it happened in the meantime that the sky became black with clouds and wind, and there was a heavy rain" (1 Kings 17:1-10 and 18:1, 41-45).

From this scripture, seven things occurred that gave Elijah the victory so that God's plans were fulfilled. Elijah did not doubt God's power to fulfill all that was spoken to him, and with unwavering faith, he walked in obedience to God's instructions.

1. Elijah heard a word from God that it would not rain except at Elijah's word. This was God's rhema or spoken word to Elijah.

2. Elijah believed the word of God which was faith.

3. Elijah spoke the word of God and told Ahab there

would not be any rain or dew. By speaking God's word, Elijah released faith for the drought to begin.

4. Elijah obeyed the word of God when God told him you go to the brook and then to the widow. This condition of obedience was needed for God's spoken word to come to pass.

5. Elijah prayed the word God gave him that the drought would end. On Mount Carmel, Elijah prayed fervently seven times for rain to begin in accordance with God's spoken word.

6. God heard the words of Elijah's prayer and formed a small cloud over the waters. There was an open heaven for God to hear because of Elijah's obedience and perseverance in prayer. He had to press into God to receive the answer.

7. God answered, and His word came to pass when the rains came in a torrential downpour.

God's word was fulfilled only because Elijah heard, believed, spoke, obeyed, and prayed. You are no different than Elijah. You hear God speak directly to you through His Word or through His Holy Spirit. You believe what He spoke, and you speak forth His promises. You obey His Word, and you pray in agreement with God. If you know Jesus as your Lord and Savior, this was the exact process you followed to become a child of God. You heard, believed, spoke, obeyed, and prayed. If you have never received Jesus as your Savior, then you are not God's child, and you do not have the assurance that heaven is your final destination. God is speaking to you right now. Will you hear? Will you believe God has revealed to you that Jesus Christ is God; He died on the cross for your sins and rose from the dead on the third day? Will you confess and repent of your sin and ask the Lord Jesus to forgive you? Will you promise to love God by obeying His commands? Will you pray in agreement with God's plans to give you eternal life in heaven? Heaven or Hell...Your Choice!

Epilogue

These are the words of the Lord Jesus Christ to those who have an ear to hear:

"Time is short. Soon I will be returning. Repent for the kingdom of God is at hand. Depart from your wicked ways. My Father in heaven is searching for hearts that are loyal to Him. When He finds a heart that is dedicated and submitted to Him, He will guard, protect, provide for, discipline, and lavishly love them."

"I have many rewards for those who diligently seek after My righteousness. The world is a dark place, and it will continue to get darker as evil takes it by force. Do not fear; for the LORD will arise over you, and His glory will be seen upon you. In these last days, many will be persecuted for My namesake and will lose their lives for the sake of the gospel. Hold fast to your faith, for in the end, you will be rewarded greatly. Stand firm! Do not waver! No eye has seen or ear has heard of the riches I have in store for those who love Me."

"I am the Alpha and the Omega, the Beginning and the End. I am the Lamb who was slain before the foundation

of the world. I am the Lion of the Tribe of Judah. I am the Good Shepherd. When I call My sheep, they know My voice. Hear Me now! Rejoice in your salvation! Again I say rejoice! Lift up your voice in joyful songs. Lift up your hands in praise. Lift up your heart in submission. And I will lift you up to My throne. Behold, I am coming quickly!"

Need
additional
copies?

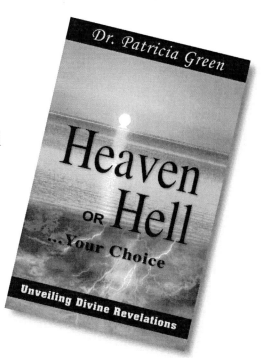

To order more copies of

Heaven or Hell...*Your Choice*

Unveiling Divine Revelations

contact NewBookPublishing.com

❐ Order online at

NewBookPublishing.com/HeavenorHell

❐ Call 877-311-5100 or

❐ Email Info@NewBookPublishing.com